A Gift for

_____

Presented by

_____

Opening Pandora's Box

Opening Pandora's Box

Phrases Borrowed
from the Classics and
the Stories behind Them

FERDIE ADDIS

The Reader's Digest Association, Inc.
New York, NY/Montreal

A READER'S DIGEST BOOK
Copyright © 2012 Michael O'Mara Books Limited
All rights reserved. Unauthorized reproduction, in any manner, is prohibited.
Reader's Digest is a registered trademark of The Reader's Digest Association, Inc.

First published in Great Britain in 2010 by Michael O'Mara Books Limited
9 Lion Yard, Tremadoc Road, London SW4 7NQ

READER'S DIGEST TRADE PUBLISHING
U.S. Project Editor: Kim Casey
Manager, English Book Editorial, Reader's Digest Canada: Pamela Johnson
Project Designers: Elizabeth Tunnicliffe, Rich Kershner
Illustrator: Andrew Pinder
Indexer: Nan Badgett
Editorial Intern: Max Bloom
Typesetting: Ed Pickford
Senior Art Director: George McKeon
Executive Editor, Trade Publishing: Dolores York
Manufacturing Manager: Elizabeth Dinda
Associate Publisher, Trade Publishing: Rosanne McManus
President and Publisher, Trade Publishing: Harold Clarke

Library of Congress Cataloging-in-Publication Data
Addis, Ferdie, 1983-
 Opening Pandora's box : phrases borrowed from the classics and the stories behind them /
Ferdie Addis.
    p. cm.
Includes index.
ISBN 978-1-60652-324-7
1. Mythology, Classical--Miscellanea. 2. English language--Terms and phrases--History. 3.
Mythology, Roman. I. Title.
BL727.A34 2012
398.0938--dc22   2011012481

We are committed to both the quality of our products and the service we provide to our
customers. We value your comments, so please feel free to contact us.
        The Reader's Digest Association, Inc.
        Adult Trade Publishing, 44 S. Broadway, White Plains, N.Y. 10601

For more Reader's Digest products and information, visit our website:
        www.rd.com (in the United States)
        www.readersdigest.ca (in Canada)

Printed in the United States of America

1 3 5 7 9 10 8 6 4 2

ACKNOWLEDGMENTS
Many thanks are due to Lindsay Davies, Kerry Chapple, Rowena Anketell and everyone at
Michael O'Mara books for their kindness and hard work. Also to Laura, Noonie and my
family for keeping me cheerful in the face of deadlines. Most of all, thanks to Valerie Mi-
nogue, whose good advice and late-night toil helped to turn a rough draft into a proper book.

"Who harkens to the gods, the gods give ear."

—HOMER, *The Iliad*

CONTENTS

Oh, my! Who was your last hairdresser?

CONTENTS

I think that he's got your eyes.

INTRODUCTION

Perhaps you're as rich as Croesus or one of the hoi polloi? Maybe you work like a Trojan or maybe you just have the Midas touch? Have you seen a pantomime, spent money, heard an echo or thought something was tragic? One thing's for sure: You'll definitely have used some of the phrases in this book.

Modern English is stuffed full of references to the mythology or history of the ancient world. Some of them are obviously of classical origin, such as "Achilles' heel," but some of them are so deeply buried that we hardly notice them at all. How many people these days realize that "ocean" comes from the Greek creation myth? What links breakfast cereal, an ancient goddess and a festival of flaming foxes? What does the word money have to do with a Gallic invasion and a gaggle of sacred geese?

These tales from the ancient world used to be part of a shared body of knowledge that ran like a golden thread through the fabric of Western culture. Artists have been inspired by myths and legends for centuries, using classical allusions to add rich layers of meaning. Writers such as Shakespeare, Milton, Tennyson and Joyce produced works that are part of a great literary conversation that stretches all the way back to ancient Greece and Rome.

But now that people have learned that there's more to a proper education than reading loads of Greek and Latin, the unfortunate side effect is that even the more famous stories are being forgotten. We remember the *Titanic* but not the Titans. We say that "the die is cast" but we don't know why Julius Caesar cast it. We feel jovial, but nobody thinks much these days about Jove.

As we lose the memory of the old myths, we lose the key that unlocks the secret meaning behind these ordinary phrases. The aim of this book is to pry open the lid of the English language, just like Pandora did with her famous box, and let the weird and wonderful stories that we used to know come blinking out again into the light of day.

How Did These Stories Start?

Most of the stories of classical mythology have roots that go back into what even the ancient Greeks would have considered to be the very distant past. As they evolved, being passed down orally from generation to generation, the stories split into a multitude of different strands and local variations. And things only got worse when poets and writers started getting involved. If a myth didn't go the way they wanted, classical authors were very happy to make their own changes or even make up a new story entirely.

That means that for almost all the myths that are retold in this book, there will be alternative versions that sometimes differ significantly from each other. In general, I have tried to choose the version that is most commonly used. However, when there's no obvious "correct" version, I've simply chosen the one that seemed most exciting; a policy which is, after all, very much in the tradition of the ancient poets.

Versions of myths come from a huge number of classical writers, but four poets in particular stand out as strong sources for a huge amount of myths and legends:

Hesiod—a very early epic poet who wrote two poems, the *Theogony* and *Works and Days,* which deal with the mythological origins of the world and mankind's place in it.

Homer—regarded by the Greeks as the father of literature, famous for two poems, the *Iliad* and the *Odyssey,* which deal with the Trojan War and the fate of the hero, Odysseus, who fought in it. It's now thought that the poems may be the work of more than one author, and that Homer may be a mythical rather than historical figure.

Ovid—another Roman poet who provided fanciful versions of many famous myths in his great poem *Metamorphoses.*

Virgil—a Roman poet, most famous for the epic poem the *Aeneid,* which tells of the adventures of Aeneas, Trojan hero and ancestor of the Roman people, after the Trojan War.

It's All (Mostly) Greek to Us

Although the gods of Greece and Rome had different names, and subtly different attributes, the two pantheons were so similar that they were generally considered by both Greeks and Romans to be the same. Roman writers retelling Greek myths would simply replace the Greek names for gods with their Latin equivalent.

In this book I've used the Greek names, except when the context is distinctively Roman. Together, the 12 main gods of Greek and Roman mythology are often called the Olympians.

THE OLYMPIAN GODS

Greek	Latin	Role
Zeus	Jupiter	King of the gods. Associated with the sky and thunder.
Hera	Juno	Queen of the gods and wife of Zeus/Jupiter. Goddess of women and marriage. Constantly annoyed with her adulterous husband.
Athena	Minerva	Goddess of war, wisdom and crafts. Daughter of Zeus/Jupiter. Especially associated with the city of Athens.
Aphrodite	Venus	Goddess of love. Julius Caesar claimed to be descended from her.
Artemis	Diana	Goddess of the moon and of hunting. A sworn virgin. Sister of Apollo.
Apollo	Apollo	God of art, medicine and prophecy. Brother of Artemis.
Hephaestus	Vulcan	The limping blacksmith god. Associated with volcanoes.
Poseidon	Neptune	God of the sea and earthquakes. Brother of Zeus/Jupiter.
Demeter	Ceres	Goddess of crops and fertility.
Hermes	Mercury	The messenger god. Associated with traders.
Dionysus	Bacchus	God of wine and vegetation. Famously wild.
Ares	Mars	God of war. More important in Rome than in Greece.

13

A

ACADEMY

An institution of higher learning or culture

The world's first academy was founded in Athens at the beginning of the fourth century B.C. by the philosopher Plato, who was perhaps one of the greatest and most influential thinkers of ancient Greece. It started as a simple association of like-minded intellectuals, which was named after its meeting place near the grove of the hero Academus on the outskirts of the city.

Through the Academy, Plato taught young Athenian aristocrats (including the equally influential philosopher Aristotle) the arts of philosophy, geometry and mathematics. Even after Plato's death, the Academy continued as a center of learning, developing ideas that would become the foundation of Western philosophy and have a profound influence on the development of Christian ideology hundreds of years later.

In modern English, the word academic has come to imply "out of touch," "pointless" or "obscure." This, of course, is terribly unfair to the original Academics, whose philosophies lie at the very heart of later Western thought.

ACHILLES' HEEL

A person's weak spot or vulnerability

Achilles' wrath, to Greece the direful spring Of
woes unnumber'd, heavenly goddess, sing!
—Homer, *Iliad,* i.1–2, trans. Alexander Pope

The story of Achilles is central to the plot of the *Iliad,* Homer's epic poem of the Trojan War and Greek literature's earliest and perhaps finest work. The poem tells what happens when Achilles quarrels with Agamemnon, his commander-in-chief, and withdraws from the fighting around Troy.

Deprived of their best fighter, the Greek army is pushed back by the Trojans until Achilles' beloved friend Patroclus enters the battle wearing the hero's famous armor. The Trojans, thinking that Achilles has returned, begin to flee, but the Trojan hero Hector kills Patroclus and stems the tide. Devastated by his friend's death, Achilles vows revenge and defeats the unfortunate Hector under the walls of Troy.

At this point, the *Iliad* ends, but Achilles became such a huge figure in the Greek world that later writers (like modern fans who write homemade sequels to *The Lord of the Rings)* kept adding to the mythology around him. It was the Roman poet Statius who introduced the story that the baby Achilles had been dipped in the River Styx. This, Statius wrote, made him invulnerable except at the heel by which his mother had held him.

In Statius's version, Achilles is finally killed by a poisoned arrow that strikes the vulnerable spot, and ever since, any fatal weakness has been called an "Achilles', heel."

ADONIS

An incredibly handsome man

Adonis is one of mythology's more mysterious figures. The ancient Greek writers can't even agree who his father was, and they generally treat him as only semidivine. On the other hand, Adonis has a long history as an object of cult worship, with deep roots in Near Eastern religion: He has strong similarities with the powerful Egyptian god Osiris, and his name comes from the same root as the Hebrew Adonai—one of the names of the God of the Old Testament.

The sources do agree, though, that Adonis was extraordinarily good-looking. At one point he had two of Greece's most powerful goddesses—Aphrodite, the goddess of love, and Persephone, the queen of the Underworld—competing for his affection. The goddesses were so smitten by the young demigod that in the end

Zeus had to step in, dividing Adonis's time equally between the two.

This exhausting arrangement was not to last. One day, when Adonis was hunting, an angry god—some say it was a jealous Ares, others that it was Artemis or Apollo—took the form of a monstrous wild boar and mortally wounded him. Aphrodite, heartbroken, watched Adonis die in her arms.

As a religious figure, Adonis was remembered in secret ceremonies attended only by women, who would plant sacred seeds and lament his untimely death.

TO BE UNDER THE AEGIS

To be under someone's protection or authority

In Greek mythology, the aegis was a very mysterious garment associated with Zeus and his daughter Athena. Sometimes the aegis is represented as a sort of cloak. At other times, it is a shield or a fringed breastplate. In some accounts it was made out of goatskin (perhaps the skin of the magical she-goat Amalthea), while others claim it was made of gold. In Athena's hands, the aegis is sometimes a mantle woven out of hissing snakes.

At any rate, the aegis was believed to be a tool of incredible power. Zeus could bring down thunderstorms and strike terror into mortals just by shaking it, and Athena wore it in battle to terrify her enemies. Set on the front of the aegis was the severed head of the Gorgon Medusa, which was so horrible to look at that anyone who saw it turned to stone.

To be covered by the aegis of the gods was to have some friends in seriously high places, and that sense of protection, coupled with high authority, survives today.

AMAZON

A fierce, tall, athletic or wild woman

The Amazons were a legendary tribe of women who were thought by the Greeks to have lived in the Caucasus Mountains on the borders of modern-day Russia (at the outer limits of the known world at the time).

Living entirely without men, Amazonian women filled all the traditionally male roles in society. According to the Greek geographer Strabo, the Amazons' only contact with adult males came either in battle or at special ceremonies convened twice a year strictly for purposes of procreation. They were thought to have been ferocious fighters. Some said that the Amazons used to burn off their right breasts so that no womanly appendage could get in the way of the bowstring or impede their spear arm.

For the ancient Greeks, these early proponents of women's lib were both scary and rather alluring. Mythological stories of the Amazons generally show them being soundly beaten by macho Greek heroes, with Theseus and Heracles both notching up victories against the warrior women. The mighty Achilles broke the mold by falling in love with the Amazon queen Penthesilea, but only after he had successfully rendered her less threatening by stabbing her to death.

Incredulous that a tribe of women "could ever be organized without men," Strabo regarded the Amazons as entirely mythical, and most modern scholars have agreed with him. However, there is some limited archaeological evidence from grave mounds of mysterious female fighters who rode the Russian steppes two and a half millennia ago. It may be that the "mythical" Amazons had a real foundation after all.

APHRODISIAC

Something that stimulates sexual desire

Aphrodisiacs are named after Aphrodite, the ancient Greek goddess of love and sex. Born from the sea foam around the castrated testicles of the sky-god Uranus, Aphrodite was the ultimate male fantasy, a perfect woman whose erotic charms nobody could resist.

She was also one of the more dangerous goddesses to annoy. Her specialty was driving her victims mad with forbidden passion before utterly destroying them. The princess Myrrha, for example, fell in love with and seduced her own father before being transformed into a myrrh tree; Theseus' wife, Phaedra, fell in love with her stepson and committed suicide; and worst of all, the Cretan queen Pasiphaë fell in love with a bull and gave birth to the hideous Minotaur, who was half man and half beast.

Even Aphrodite's favorites didn't have it easy. The Trojan hero Anchises (father of Aeneas, the legendary ancestor of the Romans) came perilously close to being destroyed by one of Zeus' thunderbolts when he dared to boast to his friends of having slept with the goddess of love. Her most famous protégé was another Trojan, Prince Paris, whom she rewarded for taking her side in a beauty contest. This "reward" turned out to be Helen, the wife of the Greek king Menelaus, who, deprived of his trophy bride, turned up with an army that eventually killed Paris and burned Troy to the ground.

APPLE OF DISCORD

Something calculated to cause a quarrel; a prize to be fought over

To the ancient Greeks, discord wasn't just an abstract idea. Discord (Eris in Greek) was a goddess of the Greek Pantheon, one of the daughters of Night, and mother of Sorrow, Forgetfulness, Disease, Murder and Massacres, and other such attractive divinities.

Unsurprisingly, Eris wasn't among the more popular immortals and so, when the minor sea spirit Thetis was getting married to the mortal hero Peleus, the quarrelsome goddess was among the few deities not to receive an invitation. In revenge for the insult, she turned up at the wedding and threw a golden apple down upon the table. On the apple was written one word: *kallistei*—"for the most beautiful."

This would have been fine if three of Greek mythology's most powerful (and vainest) goddesses hadn't been present. As Discord had predicted, a furious argument soon broke out between Hera, Athena and Aphrodite. Each goddess claimed the apple for herself, and none of the other gods was brave enough to choose between them. In the end, the three goddesses submitted to the famous Judgement of Paris, which led directly to the catastrophic violence of the Trojan War.

ARACHNID

An arthropod of the class Arachnida; a spider

According to Greek myth, the first spider was once a human girl named Arachne. She lived, the story goes, in Lydia in modern-day Turkey where she became famous for the fine quality of her weaving. This would have been all well and good had she not, in a fit of arrogance, boasted that her work was better than that of Athena.

Athena was, among other things, the patron goddess of crafts, and therefore, extremely irritated to find herself challenged by a mere mortal. Her mood did not improve when Arachne went on to make good on her bold claim. Challenged to a weaving contest by the angry deity, Arachne produced a mocking work covered in depictions of gods behaving badly. Even worse, Arachne's piece was flawless, a perfect example of the weaver's art—she'd beaten Athena at her own game.

If Arachne had known her Greek myths better, she would have known that this was extremely unwise. Furious at the girl's impertinence (but not angry enough to have forgotten her sense of irony), Athena transformed Arachne into a spider, and doomed her to weave webs for the rest of time.

ARCADIAN IDYLL

An idealized vision of rural life; a countryside paradise

Arcadia was, and still is, a mountainous region of Greece in the middle of the Peloponnese. It was a remote area with few major towns, populated mostly by shepherds with their flocks. And it was thought, in Greek mythology, to be the home of the goat god Pan and his wild followers.

For its inhabitants, Arcadia probably didn't have a lot going for it. Rural life in the classical world was always hard, and the harsh Arcadian landscape would have been particularly unforgiving. But when the Roman poet Virgil wanted a setting for a book of romantic pastoral poetry, he chose Arcadia. As the backdrop for Virgil's *Eclogues* (a collection of verses about merry herdsmen conversing in rhyme and having love affairs), Arcadia was put on the map once and for all.

Throughout the Middle Ages and the Renaissance, and even to this day, Arcadia has remained the proverbial setting for imagined rural bliss, the subject of countless poems and works of art. One of the most famous is the painting *Et in Arcadia Ego* by Nicolas Poussin, where the titular words appear as a memento mori, carved on a tomb to remind the viewer that "even in Arcadia, I [Death] exist."

ARCHIMEDES SCREW

An early mechanical device used to draw water from one place to another through a pipe

Archimedes was a philosopher and mathematician who lived in the Sicilian city of Syracuse in the third century B.C. He is regarded by modern scholars as one of the greatest mathematical thinkers ever to have lived. In many fields, Archimedes' insights weren't improved on until the invention of calculus, more than a thousand years later.

The Romans learned the hard way to respect Archimedes' science when they sent a fleet to capture Syracuse during the Second Punic War. To repel the attacking fleet, Archimedes is said to have deployed a formidable arsenal of war machines, including enormous lever-operated grappling cranes, which were able to pluck the Roman galleys right out of the sea.

Compared to these technological marvels, the Archimedes screw is a modest device, essentially just a tube with a corkscrew in the middle, useful for drawing water from low-lying ponds into irrigation canals or cisterns. It may not even have been invented by Archimedes.

Nonetheless, it's fitting that the philosopher gave his name to a peaceful tool rather than a war machine. When Syracuse finally fell, the Roman soldiers found him, not on the walls brandishing a sword, but calmly writing equations in the sand, so distracted by the beauty of his math that he had entirely forgotten the battle.

ARGONAUT

A sailor undertaking an adventurous or perilous voyage

One of Greek mythology's most popular stories tells of the quest of the hero Jason to retrieve the legendary Golden Fleece. This fleece, with solid gold wool, was hidden in the kingdom of Colchis, at the eastern end of the Black Sea, on the fringe of what the Greeks thought of as the civilized world.

To make this dangerous voyage, Jason assembled a crew that included all the greatest heroes of the day. Heracles, Orpheus, Castor, Pollux, Theseus and a host of others joined the expedition in the hope of plunder or glory. Together they were known as the "Argonauts," from *Argo,* the name of their ship, and *nautês,* meaning "sailor" (the root of words, such as astronaut and nautical).

Jason did succeed in stealing the Golden Fleece from Colchis, but it certainly wasn't easy. By the time the Argonauts returned to Greece, they had faced pitched battles, wild boars, Harpies, Sirens, Scylla and Charybdis, lustful nymphs, fire-breathing bulls, murderous Lemnian women, clashing rocks and men grown from dragon's teeth. Their voyage had taken them most of the way around the Mediterranean and the Black Sea.

TO BE ARGUS-EYED

To be watchful or alert

In Greek mythology, Argus was a giant who had a hundred eyes, all looking in different directions. The goddess Hera employed him as a watchman to guard the nymph Io, who had been transformed into a gleaming white heifer. Hera's husband, Zeus, had fallen deeply in love with the bovine nymph, but with Argus constantly on the lookout, it was impossible for the great god to pursue his adulterous passion.

Argus was the perfect watchman—he could see in all directions, and he only slept with half of his eyes closed at a time. Eventually, the frustrated Zeus sent the messenger-god Hermes to dispose of the troublesome herdsman. Despite all his strength, Argus was no match for a true immortal. In retribution for the killing of her servant, Hera sent a gadfly, which stung Io, harrying her around the Ionian Sea, which bears her name, across the Bosphorus (Greek for "cow crossing") and all the way to Egypt, where she became the goddess Isis. Poor dead Argus never achieved such fame, but his hundred eyes and watchful nature have made his name a popular title for local newspapers.

FAITHFUL ARGUS

Someone who is very faithful, especially a dog or pet

The Greek hero Odysseus spent 10 years far away from his home, fighting in the Trojan War, and it took him 10 years after that to make the long journey back again. By the time he returned, he had been given up for dead, and his palace had been taken over by a group of local young men who were all trying to marry his wife.

Because of these rowdy suitors, Odysseus was forced to enter his home in disguise, dressed as an old beggar. However, his cover was almost blown right away when he saw his old hound Argus lying neglected on a dung heap. This dog, whom Odysseus had raised as a pup before he left, had been waiting 20 years for his master to return. Recognizing Odysseus despite his beggar's rags, Argus lifted his tired head, gave a happy whimper, and died on the spot.

> The dog, whom fate had granted to behold His lord,
> when twenty tedious years had roll'd Takes a last
> look and having seen him, dies; So closed for ever
> faithful Argus' eyes!
> —Homer, *Odyssey*, trans. Alexander Pope, bk. xvii

ARISTOPHANIC HUMOR

Surreal or crude humor in the style of Aristophanes

Aristophanes (*c.* 445 to *c.* 385 B.C.) was an Athenian playwright from Greece's Classical era. He was considered the finest writer of "Old Comedy" by later critics, and since he's the only Old Comedian whose work has survived, we have to take their word for it.

Aristophanes' plays are rude, irreverent and often deal with fantastical or impossible situations. In *The Frogs,* the god Dionysus travels to the Underworld to bring back the soul of a tragic playwright. *In Peace,* an Athenian travels to heaven on a dung beetle in order to prosecute the gods. Most outlandish of all, by ancient Greek standards, is the *Lysistrata,* which sees women taking over the city of Athens by going on a sex strike.

These strange plots were vehicles for Aristophanes to do what he loved best: squeeze in as many jokes about sex, death and bodily functions as he possibly could, while making up long nonsense words and being outrageously rude about the prominent Athenians of the day. Aristophanes' version of the philosopher Socrates, in his play *The Clouds,* was so grotesque that the real Socrates felt compelled to stand up in front of the audience to try to remind them what he was really like.

IN THE ARMS OF MORPHEUS

Asleep

Morpheus was one of the many divine sons of the Greek god Hypnos, or Sleep. According to Ovid's *Metamorphoses,* Morpheus lived with his brothers and his father in a pitch-black cave in a sacred mountain somewhere near the Crimea. From this cave, Sleep would dispatch his sons to appear in people's dreams. Some would appear only as inanimate objects. Others were restricted to appearing in the dreams of peasants or slaves and probably became very good at impersonating favorite cows or grumpy fishwives.

Among this motley cast, Morpheus was the big star. He only appeared in the dreams of heroes, kings and the nobility. His skill at conjuring up new forms for himself is what gave him his name, from the Greek *morphê,* meaning "shape." Nowadays this spirit of sleep and hallucination is probably best known through the drug to which he gave his name: the psychoactive anesthetic morphine.

ATLAS'S SHOULDERS

Shoulders capable of bearing a great weight or responsibility, like those of Atlas

Atlas was one of the giants, a race of monstrous beings blessed with superhuman strength and power. Children of the goddess Gaia, the giants rebelled against the Olympian gods and caused chaos before finally being defeated. For his part in the battle, Atlas was condemned to an extraordinary punishment. His job, for all eternity, was to stand like a gigantic pillar and hold up the sky.

In the end, Atlas was relieved of this awful task by the hero Perseus, who passed by on his way home with the famous Gorgon's head. Feeling sorry for the tortured giant, Perseus allowed Atlas to look at the Gorgon's face, which was so horrible that he immediately turned to stone, becoming the Atlas mountain range.

A famous early set of world maps featured the figure of Atlas on the front, holding up a globe. Since then, the word atlas has been used to describe any collection of maps.

ATOMS AND ELEMENTS

The fundamental building blocks of physics and chemistry

The modern table of elements was first invented by Antoine Lavoisier in the eighteenth century, but the idea of an "element"—a substance that can't be separated into constituent parts—has been a part of Western thought since the Greek philosopher Empedocles in the fifth century B.C. According to him, the universe was composed of four basic elements: earth, air, fire and water. Remarkably, this basic list would be widely accepted for more than two thousand years.

But not all ancient Greeks bought the theory. While Empedocles was cooking up the theory of elements, the famous Thracian philosophers Leucippus and Democritus were developing the idea of the "atom," a tiny indivisible particle of matter named from the Greek *atomos,* or "uncuttable." These atoms, floating in the void, were the basis for the entire material world.

As scientific knowledge began to expand in early modern Europe, the idea of atoms as nature's most fundamental building blocks began to gain new popularity. By the time Ernest Rutherford split the "unsplittable" atom at the beginning of the twentieth century, the inappropriate name had stuck.

▣ B ▣

BACCHANALIAN ORGY

A wild party where the normal rules don't apply

Bacchus, or Dionysus as he was also known, was the god of wine, drama, vegetation and ritual madness. With his retinue of Maenads and Bacchantes, Satyrs and Centaurs, he traveled around Greece and Asia causing chaos wherever he went and indulging in wild "orgies"—a word that the ancient Greeks used to describe secret rituals rather than the sex parties that the term implies today.

Not that the Bacchanalian orgies were tame affairs. The most famous "bacchanal" of Greek mythology is recorded in *The Bacchae*, a play by the great Athenian playwright Euripides. In the play, Bacchus arrives in Thebes where his mortal cousin King Pentheus has banned the citizens from celebrating the Bacchic rites. However, the Theban women, under Bacchus' spell, defy their king's ban and join the god up in the mountains. Even the king's mother, Agave, goes to join the revelers, and in the end, Pentheus decides to sneak up the mountain to see what all the fuss is about.

Predictably, the encounter between the peeping king and the maddened followers of an angry god does not end well. The Theban women, in the grip of divine frenzy, tear the unfortunate Pentheus to bloody pieces. As for Agave, it's not until she returns to the city that she realizes that the hunting trophy she's carrying in her arms is the gory remnant of her own son's severed head.

In the 1600s the word orgy began to take on its modern meaning, when early modern writers, fantasizing about the thrilling debauchery of ancient religion, began to use the term to describe any particularly riotous revelry or party.

BARBARIAN

Someone with no culture or civilization; a brute

The ancient Greeks invented the word *barbaros* to describe basically any foreigner. The incomprehensible babble of foreign language sounded, they thought, like someone repeatedly saying, "bar bar bar." Unlike the Greeks, who lived under the rule of law and were properly civilized in their customs, barbarians, like the Persians or the Romans, were thought to live lives of total moral squalor and corruption.

The pain of seeming barbaric to the Greeks did little to discourage the Romans from applying the very same word to the many foreign peoples they encountered on their road to an empire. Unlike the virtuous Romans, barbarians, like the Gauls, could be found doing all sorts of odd things: painting themselves with woad, human sacrifice, even wearing pants!

Of course, the "barbarian" people were generally nothing of the sort. The nations at the periphery of the classical world often had cultures every bit as rich and evolved as the snobbish Greeks and Romans.

BELLEROPHONIC LETTER

A message intended to do harm to its bearer

Bellerophon was a Corinthian prince, famous in Greek mythology for killing the monstrous Chimera. The story of how he ended up fighting the Chimera in the first place is less well known.

According to the legend, Bellerophon was staying at the palace of King Proetus when the king's wife, Stheneboea, tried to seduce him. When Bellerophon rejected her advances, the jilted queen took her revenge by secretly telling her husband the king that his heroic guest had tried to rape her.

The next day, Proetus sent Bellerophon away carrying a mysterious letter addressed to another local king called Iobates. This letter was duly delivered, but Iobates must have been surprised to see that it contained only a request that its bearer be immediately put to death.

But killing Bellerophon was easier said than done. Iobates tried the traditional trick of giving the hero seemingly impossible tasks (including fighting the Chimera), but Bellerophon succeeded at them all. An ambush by Iobates' best warriors also failed when Bellerophon held them all off single-handedly. Eventually, Iobates was forced to concede that the gods were on Bellerophon's side and gave up trying to kill him.

TO BESTRIDE SOMETHING LIKE A COLOSSUS

To be a giant in some field; to be preeminent

Why, man, he doth bestride the narrow world
Like a Colossus, and we petty men Walk under
his huge legs and peep about To find ourselves
dishonorable graves.
        —Shakespeare, *Julius Caesar,* I.ii.135-8

The Colossus of Rhodes was a huge statue of the sun god Helios, built by the grateful citizens in memory of their victory at the Siege of Rhodes in 304 B.C. The attacking army, led by Demetrius "the Besieger" Poliorcetes, deployed a machine called the Helepolis, an ironclad tower mounted with catapults, which could be wheeled up to the city walls to allow attackers to fire down onto the defenders below.

But the Rhodians cleverly flooded the land over which this daunting contraption had to travel. Weighed down by its armor, it stuck fast in the mud and had to be abandoned. When Demetrius finally gave up the siege and sailed away, the Rhodians had the Helepolis melted down and used the metal to build a 98-foot (30-meter) high statue dedicated to their patron god.

This Colossus stood overlooking their harbor until it was destroyed by an earthquake in 224 B.C. Although nothing is now left of the statue, it was considered to be one of the Seven Wonders of the ancient world and remains a potent symbol of superhuman grandeur.

BEWARE THE GREEKS BEARING GIFTS

Don't trust your enemies, even when they appear to be acting in your interest

This phrase is a reference to a line in Virgil's *Aeneid,* part of the debate over what ought to be done with the famous Trojan Horse.

This horse was a mysterious wooden statue that had been left behind outside the city of Troy by the retreating Greek army. Many Trojans believed the horse was a holy object and should be brought within the walls. However, the priest Laocoön reminded the Trojans not to trust the Greeks whom they'd fought for so long, saying: *"Timeo Danaos et dona ferentes"*—"I fear the Greeks, even when they bring gifts." This Latin phrase is still sometimes used with the same meaning as the more familiar English version.

Laocoön was right not to trust the Greeks or their "gift," but the goddess Athena, who was firmly on the Greek side, soon interrupted his doomed protestations. Her method—crude but effective—was to summon up a pair of sea serpents who crushed the unfortunate priest to death and even ate his two sons for good measure.

The Trojans, intimidated by this show of divine anger, dragged the horse into the city. By the time they discovered that its hollow belly was full of Greek soldiers, it was too late.

BEWARE THE IDES OF MARCH

Watch out for unseen dangers, even when things seem to be going well

In the Roman calendar, the "Ides" was the name given to a day around the middle of each month from which other dates were calculated. The Ides of March, 44 B.C. is famous as the date when

Julius Caesar, then the undisputed master of the Roman world, was assassinated.

According to the ancient biographer Plutarch, Caesar was warned by a soothsayer, or prophet, to beware of disaster on the Ides of March. When the day arrived, he happened to meet the soothsayer again on his way through the Roman Forum and mockingly said, "Look, the Ides of March have come." The soothsayer replied, "Yes, but they have not yet gone." Soon afterward, Julius Caesar, dictator of Rome, was murdered in cold blood by a group of his supposed friends.

BREAD AND CIRCUSES

Handouts aimed at securing the support of an apathetic populace; the petty concerns of the politically disengaged

The Roman satirist Juvenal, writing around A.D. 100, invented the phrase "bread and circuses" as a damning indictment of the state of the Roman citizens of his era. Whereas the citizens of the Republic (which crumbled about a century and a half before Juvenal was writing) had exercised their voting rights with pride, solemnly choosing magistrates and generals to rule over them, the modern population of Rome would elect whoever bribed them the most. Modern Romans, Juvenal complained, only cared about two things: bread (the free grain ration that was handed out to the poor of the city) and circuses (the vast gladiatorial shows and other entertainment that were provided by all serious political candidates).

Ever since Juvenal, political elites have been using the phrase to express snooty despair about the foolishnesses of ordinary voters. On the other hand, some might say that bread-and-circus-loving ordinary voters actually have the right idea. Certainly in Juvenal's time, most Romans had correctly sussed out that, whomever they elected, the emperor was always going to be the real man in charge. Were they cynical, or just sensible, to decide that the best they were going to get from the whole voting business was a bit of free entertainment?

TO BURN ONE'S BOATS

To put oneself in a position from which there is no going back

In the ancient world, in which land travel was difficult and dangerous and where kingdoms lay scattered around the edges of the Mediterranean, military success often depended on control of the sea. An army traveling by ship could move straight to the heart of enemy territory, bypassing the many dangers of a long march overland.

Of course, an army that attacked by sea had to be very careful to protect its boats. If the boats were lost, the attacking army would have no escape route, and defeat would mean annihilation. In Homer's *Iliad,* perhaps the fiercest fight is the battle at the ships, where the Trojans, who at that point have the upper hand, try to set the Greek fleet ablaze to cut off their escape.

On the other hand, some commanders are said to have burned their boats as a motivational tool. The earliest recorded incident concerns Agathocles of Syracuse, who in 310 B.C. sailed his army to Carthage in Africa before burning his boats as an offering to the goddess Demeter. With no way to get back to Sicily, his soldiers knew that the price of failure would be death.

Today the expression is also often known as "to burn one's bridges"—in other words, to commit yourself to an irreversible course of action.

BYZANTINE REGULATIONS

Rules or regulations that are extremely complex or arcane

By the third century A.D. the vast Roman Empire was beginning to tear apart under its own weight. With barbarians pressing at all the frontiers, from the deserts of Iraq to the cold fringes of Scotland, there were just too many battles for one emperor to fight.

To try and solve this problem, the emperor Diocletian divided the empire into two halves. The Western Empire, ruled by his co-emperor Maximian, included Italy, France, Britain, Spain and Africa. The Eastern Empire, which Diocletian kept for himself, held the rich territories of the ancient Greek and Hellenistic states and stretched from the Danube in the west to the distant Euphrates on the Persian border.

In A.D. 476 the last of the Western Emperors, Romulus Augustus, was deposed by a "barbarian" king, but while Rome was crumbling in the West, the Eastern Empire was flourishing. With a new capital at Constantinople, built on the site of the old Greek port of Byzantium, this "Byzantine" Empire would preserve the legacy of the Caesars for another thousand years. In the process, it would develop an imperial bureaucracy whose complexity would become proverbial.

C

CAESAREAN SECTION

*An operation where a baby is delivered through
a surgical incision in the womb*

According to popular belief, the lifesaving operation known as the Caesarean section received its name because the baby Julius Caesar was delivered by being cut out of his mother's womb. Roman surgeons certainly did have the knowledge to carry out such an operation—in fact, Caesarean sections were far from unheard of in the ancient world. However, we can be pretty sure that Julius Caesar's mother (who lived to see her son's fortieth birthday) didn't have one. Although babies were known to survive the procedure, mothers never did.

In fact, although "Caesar" and "Caesarean" are linked, "Caesarean" is probably derived from the Latin verb *caedere,* "to cut." As for "Caesar," it was an ancient family name of the Julian clan to which Julius Caesar belonged. Pliny the Elder claimed that some forgotten ancestor of the Caesars was born by Caesarean, but it's just as likely that the name comes from *caesaries,* meaning "a head of hair." For poor old Julius, who was notoriously bald, this would have been a very cruel irony.

CAESAR'S WIFE MUST BE ABOVE SUSPICION

For some people, even being suspected of wrongdoing is unacceptable, whether they're innocent or not

This phrase refers to one of the great scandals of Roman history, which broke in 62 B.C. when Publius Clodius Pulcher disguised himself as a woman so he could sneak into the house of Pompeia, the wife of Julius Caesar. At the time, Pompeia and some of her female friends were performing the sacred rites of the goddess Bona Dea, a secret ceremony that could only be attended by women. To have a man in the house at the same time was considered an awful sacrilege, so Clodius's intrusion was doubly shocking to Roman sensibilities.

Society gossips were sure that Clodius and Pompeia must have been lovers, but Julius Caesar officially claimed to believe that his wife was innocent. At Clodius's trial, he surprised the world by refusing to testify against the man who had so shockingly invaded his wife's inner sanctum.

But despite Caesar's show of trust, he immediately divorced his unfortunate wife. Why, he was asked, had he divorced her if she'd done nothing wrong? The answer came: "I thought that my wife ought to be above suspicion."

CALENDAR

A system for dividing and measuring the passing of time over a year

In the ancient Roman calendar, each month had a *Kalends* on the 1st, a *Nones* on the 5th or 7th, and an "Ides" on the 13th or the 15th. If a Roman wanted to arrange a feast or a meeting, he used these three landmark days to name a date—for example: "the fourth day after the *Ides*" or "two days before the *Kalends*."

From the Roman *Kalends* we get the modern word calendar. In fact, our system of 12 months in a year with a leap day every fourth February is directly inherited from the system of ancient Rome. Even the names of the months, after more than two thousand years, have remained the same.

THE MONTHS OF THE YEAR

January—Januarius, named after the Roman god Janus, god of doorways and therefore, the New Year

February—Februarius, named after the Februa, a Roman purification festival held on February 15th each year

March—Martius, named after Mars, god of war

April—Aprilis, sacred to Venus; the name is probably derived from Aphrodite

May—perhaps named after the maiores, or ancestors, or after the goddess Maia

June—perhaps named after the iuniores, or the young, or after the goddess Juno

July—named after Julius Caesar, who reformed the ancient Roman ten-month calendar to make the modern 12-month "Julian calendar"

August—named after the first emperor Augustus

September—previously the seventh month; named after the Latin septem, or seven

October—from octo, eight

November—from novem, nine

December—from decem, ten

CASSANDRA

*A pessimist; someone who correctly predicts disaster
but is never believed*

Cassandra was one of the daughters of King Priam of Troy, and the victim of a more than usually cruel form of divine punishment. Apollo, god of prophecy and divination, had granted her the power to see the future. However, when she rejected his advances, he added a bitter twist: Although her predictions were always true, they would never be believed.

This was especially unfortunate because Cassandra was about to live through the terrible carnage of the Trojan War. Besieged for ten years in the city of Troy, Cassandra could foresee the deaths of her brothers Hector and Paris, the deception of the Trojan Horse, the destruction of her home, the slaughter of her father Priam, and her own abduction and rape by the conquering Greeks.

At every stage, the unfortunate prophetess was able to warn those around her of the impending catastrophe, but because of Apollo's curse, nobody she spoke to ever took her good advice. Eventually Troy was destroyed and Cassandra was taken as a slave by the brutish Agamemnon, high king of the Greeks—a grim fate that the unlucky princess had, of course, already foreseen.

CATHARSIS

Emotional purging or cleansing

The Greek word *katharsis* originally simply meant cleansing or purification. It was mainly used as a medical term until the philosopher Aristotle adopted the word to describe the effect on audiences of watching tragic plays. Plato had famously argued that tragic drama, which was hugely popular in ancient Athens, misled audiences and was corrosive to the public morals. Aristotle's work argued the opposite. Tragedy, he wrote, by evoking pity and fear, could produce a "catharsis" in its audience, which would lead to a more moral society, not less.

What exactly Aristotle meant by his "catharsis" remains the subject of philosophical debate. Is catharsis a purging of negative emotions, or is it, more subtly, a sort of internal recalibration? Presumably most Athenians didn't mind too much one way or the other—as long as they could keep going to the theater to watch their favorite gory scenes of mythology, they were content.

CATONIAN SEVERITY

Strict and uncompromising adherence to puritanical and austere values; to be a killjoy

Marcus Porcius Cato (234–149 B.C.), known as Cato the Censor, was a general, historian and statesman who was prominent in Rome at the height of the Republican period. This was a time of great change: Hannibal had been defeated; Roman power was spreading across the Mediterranean; and the nation that had begun as a modest Italian republic of citizen farmers was beginning to get a taste for the luxuries and trappings of an empire.

As wealth from the conquered provinces flooded into the city of Rome, some aristocratic families began to show signs of deviating from the strict path of Roman virtue. They wore flashy clothes and ate fancy food at expensive dinner parties. They associated with Greek philosophers and read Greek literature. Some had even started to show signs of respecting women.

C

Against these troubling tendencies, Cato stood as a beacon of old-fashioned propriety. He lived a life of ostentatious austerity, wrote treatises about farming (including advice to keep slaves working constantly, and not to bother feeding any who got sick), and was decently unpleasant to his wife. Best of all, since he'd been appointed to the Roman office of Censor, with a special mandate to improve public morals, Cato was able to impose his strict code on everybody else, too.

A SOP TO CERBERUS

*An appeasement or bribe; a small price paid
to avoid severe discomfort*

In Greek mythology, Cerberus was the guardian of the Underworld; a giant three-headed dog with a serpent's tail who watched the entrance and made sure that the living didn't enter the land of the dead or vice versa.

Cerberus certainly wasn't a monster to be taken lightly. On the other hand, for those who had the know-how, the infernal hound could prove to be a remarkably soft touch. Heracles was able to wrestle Cerberus into submission; Orpheus charmed him with the music of his harp; and most embarrassingly of all, the Trojan hero Aeneas avoided Cerberus's attention by feeding him a drugged honey cake.

Inspired by this example, ordinary Greeks and Romans sometimes buried their loved ones with little cakes or pastries distract the dozy guard dog—a custom that gives us the modern expression "a sop to Cerberus" for any small bribe.

CEREALS

Edible cultivated plants of the grass family,
now the world's most important staple food

Our word cereal is derived from the name of one of mythology's quieter deities: the ancient corn goddess Ceres. Like the plants that share her name, Ceres was modest and unassuming, and generally not thought to be of much account until the Romans—trying their hardest to look more Greek and civilized—decided that their Ceres was really the same person as the very important Greek goddess Demeter.

Boosted by this link, Ceres became one of the major deities of ancient Rome, with her own festival, the Cerialia, celebrated in April each year. As well as games in the Circus Maximus, the event featured a bizarre ritual in which foxes were released into the crowd with burning torches tied to their tails. Apart from the cruelty involved, these poor animals must have posed something of a fire hazard.

Flaming foxes aside, Ceres was, by and large, a mild and benevolent goddess. Her temple on the Aventine Hill was a refuge for the Roman poor, and a sanctuary for the oppressed. Even her sacrifices were comparatively low key: While other gods demanded the slaughter of endless cattle and sheep at their altars, Ceres was traditionally kept happy by the gift of a dry millet cake.

CHIMERA

A wild, unrealistic idea; an illusion

The Chimera was a monster from Greek mythology, which had three heads: a lion head at the front, a dragon or serpent head at the back, and in the middle a goat head that breathed fire.

The man who finally killed this extraordinary beast was the hero Bellerophon, who got within striking distance by approaching from above on the winged horse Pegasus.

Bellerophon's secret weapon was a lump of lead attached to the tip of his spear, which he stabbed into the Chimera's open mouth. There, heated by its fiery breath, the lead melted, running down its throat and putting an end to this most improbable of monsters.

In the first century A.D., the Roman orator Cicero asked, "Who now believes in Chimeras? Time destroys the inventions of the imagination, but confirms the judgments of nature and truth." The Chimera was already becoming a byword for anything that stretches the bounds of credulity just a bit too far.

CHORUS OF DISAPPROVAL

A crowd of voices united in objecting to something

The word chorus comes from the Greek *khoros*, meaning "dance" or "group of dancers." In the ancient world, choruses of between 10 and 20 men or women would perform lyric poetry and dance in honor of the gods at religious festivals or ceremonies.

These choral entertainments evolved into full-scale ancient Greek dramas, with two or three main actors playing parts on stage, while the chorus provided interludes of singing and dancing. They also had a dramatic role, as powerless observers commenting on and responding to the action. While the tragic leads on stage fight, murder each other, lust after the wrong women and go completely mad, it is the job of the chorus to stand on the sidelines protesting its impotent disapproval.

CICERONIAN ELOQUENCE

Exceptional skill at public speaking

Marcus Tullius Cicero (106–43 B.C.) was a Roman philosopher and statesman who rose to prominence through his exceptional gift for public speaking.

In both Greece and Rome, jury trials were rowdy affairs, and a good rabble-rousing speech could win even the unlikeliest of cases. Cicero quickly became a master in the law courts and a terror to his enemies, who dreaded being exposed to his brilliant and biting tongue.

Before long, Cicero's gift was propelling him into politics, and by 63 B.C. he had been elected to the consulship, Rome's highest office. For a minor provincial nobleman, this was a huge personal triumph, but the glory days of the Roman Republic were coming to an end. Elected officials like Cicero were being overshadowed by rich generals like Caesar and Pompey and the specter of violence and civil war grew more threatening by the year.

When conflict came, Cicero repeatedly picked the losing side, first attacking the victorious Caesar and then his successor, Mark Antony, in a string of brilliant and ferocious speeches. At last, the patience of the generals wore thin and Cicero was executed by Antony's soldiers. The head that had so eloquently attacked the new regime, and the hand that had written so powerfully against it, were hacked off Cicero's dead body, and nailed to the speaker's platform in the Forum.

ROMAN NAMES

Like most Roman aristocrats, Cicero had three names—a praenomen, a nomen and a cognomen. The praenomen was a personal name like a modern first name. The nomen was the family name. Last of all, the cognomen was a sort of additional surname, which could be earned or inherited. Many cognomina started off as nicknames, often unflattering. Some of the most famous belong to:

Gaius Julius Caesar—"Caesar" may come from a Latin word meaning "hairy," or an African word for elephant, among other possibilities

Gnaeus Pompeius Strabo—Strabo in Latin means "Squinty"

Marcus Tullius Cicero—Cicero comes from the Latin for chickpea. The historian Plutarch claims that one of Cicero's ancestors got the name because of an unsightly chickpealike deformity on his nose.

Publius Cornelius Scipio Africanus—named "Africanus" for his success in defeating the African Hannibal

---

TO CLEANSE THE AUGEAN STABLES

To clean up a filthy mess by drastic means

In Greek mythology, the Augean Stables were the cattle sheds of Augeas, king of Elis. Augeas's herds were so vast that they filled the sheds with unimaginable quantities of filth and manure, so much that the Augean Stables became notorious throughout Greece.

No one could be persuaded to go anywhere near the disgusting mess until the hero Heracles turned up at Augeas's palace promising to clean out the entire stables in one day. In return he demanded one-tenth of Augeas's famous cattle.

Augeas thought it would be impossible to shift the mountains of muck from the stables in one day, so he happily agreed to let the hero try. He had, however, critically underestimated Heracles, for whom the impossible was all in a day's work.

Rather than getting to work with a shovel and broom, as Augeas had expected, the brawny hero dammed up two local rivers and diverted their waters through Augeas's palace wall, and straight into the stables. The monstrous heap of slurry that had accumulated over the years was washed away in a single afternoon.

CLEOPATRA'S NOSE

A small detail that has a huge effect on subsequent events

Cleopatra was a Greco-Egyptian queen, and the last person to rule Egypt as a pharaoh before it became a Roman province in 30 B.C. By the time Cleopatra came to the throne, Egypt's power was on the wane and the frontiers of the Roman Empire were getting closer every year.

So when Julius Caesar arrived in Egypt in 48 B.C., the young Cleopatra spared no effort in getting close to the powerful general.

C

GREAT WOMEN OF THE ANCIENT WORLD

Ancient society was harsh and chauvinistic. By and large, women in the classical world were invisible—hidden away behind the doors of their marital homes. But even in this unpromising climate, some women did achieve fame and power, generally those on the fringes of the Greek and Roman worlds:

Aspasia—Greek courtesan, famously intelligent and wise; became mistress of the great Athenian leader Pericles

Boudicca (Boadicea)—queen of the Iceni tribe of East Anglia; led a dramatic rebellion against Roman rule in Britain

Cleopatra—last pharaoh of Egypt; famous for seducing Roman generals

Hypatia—Alexandrian scholar and mathematician in late antiquity; torn to pieces by an outraged Christian mob

Livia—wife of the emperor Augustus; Romans gossiped that she was the power behind the throne

Zenobia—queen of the desert city Palmyra; established a short-lived but successful independent empire in the Roman East, before finally being defeated by the emperor Aurelian

---

The biographer Plutarch relates how the queen had herself wrapped up in a carpet, which was then delivered to Caesar as a gift. Before long, the pair were lovers and Cleopatra was happily planning her future as mistress of the Roman world.

Julius Caesar's assassination four years later put an end to these happy visions, but, not to be dissuaded, Cleopatra seduced Caesar's loyal friend, Mark Antony. This time, though, she had backed the wrong horse. Antony and Cleopatra led a combined Egyptian and Roman fleet against his rival Augustus at the battle of Actium, but they were soundly beaten. The defeated queen is said to have taken her own life by exposing herself to the bite of a poisonous asp.

By seducing Antony and leading him to confrontation with Augustus, Cleopatra had a huge impact on the subsequent history of the Western world. This led the French thinker Blaise Pascal to remark that if only Cleopatra's nose had been shorter (and therefore, less attractive) the whole face of the world would have changed.

CLOUD CUCKOO LAND

Never-Never Land; an imagined ideal world that obviously doesn't exist

Cloud Cuckoo Land is the English translation of the Greek *Nephelokokkugia,* a fictional city in the sky that was invented by the Greek comedian Aristophanes for his play *The Birds.*

In the play, two Athenians find themselves in the land of the birds and inspire their new feathered friends to build a perfect city in the sky, free from the meddling of gods or men. Like many Aristophanic plays, *The Birds* offers a fantastical, impossible vision that contrasts with the harsh reality of wartime Athens, where the play was performed.

CORINTHIAN

Someone devoted to loose living, especially sports and gambling; a man about town

The ancient city of Corinth was one of the most important Greek city-states of the Classical age. It owed its prosperity partly to its remarkable position, commanding the thin neck of land that joins the Peloponnese in the south to the Greek mainland in the north and its easy sea access to both East and West. Sitting at the heart of a web of ancient trade routes, with a good harbor and a strong, defensible citadel, Corinth emerged from the "dark-ages" of 1100–900 B.C. as a thriving hub of commerce and crafts.

Over the years that followed, Corinth gained a reputation for fast living and luxury. Unlike the stern Spartans to the south and the squabbling Athenians to the north, the Corinthians were willing to put their wealth to use in the pursuit of pleasure. The city became famous for its courtesans, and the Corinthian temple of Aphrodite may have featured as many as a thousand sacred prostitutes, who would sell their bodies in the service of the goddess. Corinth became, quite literally, a byword for sex: The verb *korinthiazomai* comes up in Aristophanes, meaning (as the Victorian lexicographers primly put it) "to practice fornication."

CORNUCOPIA

An inexhaustible supply of good things;
an extraordinary abundance

The Cornucopia, from the Latin *cornu copiae* (meaning "horn of plenty"), was a magical horn that had the power to provide endless food and drink to whoever held it. The myth of its origin has several variations, but all of them agree that the horn was blessed by Zeus when he first became king of the gods.

Before Zeus was born, the chief god was a titan called Cronus, who had been told that one of his offspring would overthrow him. To prevent this, the anxious deity took the extreme step of eating all his own children the moment they were born.

Zeus was the last of these children. However, his mother, understandably tired of seeing her babies cannibalized, hid the infant god away in a remote forest, where he was looked after by two nymphs and suckled by a goat called Amalthea. When Zeus reached adulthood, he acknowledged Amalthea's service by breaking off one of her horns, which he gave as a gift to the nymphs who had guarded him. This horn, he decreed, would always be overflowing with food and drink and whatever good things a person might want.

TO CROSS THE RUBICON

To pass the point of no return; to take the plunge

The Rubicon was the name of a small river, now lost, that flowed through northern Italy. In Roman law, the Rubicon was the official boundary between Italy and the provinces.

In 49 B.C., Julius Caesar crossed the Rubicon into Italy, leading his army of veteran legionaries toward the city of Rome. It was a moment of huge significance in Roman history. By marching across Italy's sacred boundary at the head of an army, Caesar was declaring war on his own homeland, lighting the fuse on the explosive mix of conflicting ambitions and political intrigue that Rome had become.

As Caesar crossed the river, he famously said *"alea iacta est"*—"the die is cast"—to mark the beginning of his final gamble. Five years later, Julius Caesar was dead, but the civil war he had unleashed was in full swing. By the time it ended, nearly two decades after the Rubicon was crossed, Rome's Republican age was over and the Imperial age had begun.

TO CUT THE GORDIAN KNOT

To solve a complicated and difficult problem by decisive action

In Greek mythology, the Gordian knot was a knot so complex that no one could untie it. It lay in the city of Gordium in western Turkey, where a local oracle had foretold that anyone who could untie the knot would become the ruler of Asia. Unsurprisingly, the knot attracted a steady stream of people coming to try their luck.

Eventually, the story goes, this knotty problem was solved by Alexander the Great while on his way to invade the Persian Empire. Alexander studied the tangled strands briefly before hitting upon an easy solution. He simply pulled out his sword, and cut the knot in half.

To the assembled Gordians, this probably looked like the lowest form of cheating, but Alexander went on to prove the prophecy right when his small army of Macedonian pikemen cut to the heart of the crumbling Persian Empire with almost nonchalant ease. The vast and impossible armies of the East crumbled before Alexander's sword in a manner reminiscent of the Gordian knot. The oracle's prediction had proved correct.

CYCLOPEAN WALLS

Walls made of giant blocks of stone;
masonry on a superhuman scale

In Greek mythology, the Cyclopes were a race of one-eyed giants, some of whom had existed since the earliest years of the mythological world. In fact, it was the Cyclopes who were said to have provided Zeus with the thunderbolts that he used to overthrow his father Cronus at the beginning of the Olympian age.

Many years later in the mythological chronology, the hero

Odysseus met the Cyclops Polyphemus on his voyage home from Troy. Unfortunately for Odysseus, Polyphemus had developed a taste for human flesh, and the hero and his men spent some uncomfortable nights trapped at the back of the Cyclops' cave, wondering which of them would be the giant's next snack, before they were able to get away.

Cyclopes were also thought to be responsible for the vast ruins that dotted the ancient Greek landscape. These were the remains of the cities and monuments of the Mycenaean civilization, which had flourished as much as a millennium before the Classical age of Greek culture. To the Classical Greeks, the Mycenaean walls with their giant stones looked like the work of superhumans, and they came to be known as "cyclopean."

CYNICAL INDIFFERENCE

A jaded or negative attitude to life and society

In the ancient world, the Cynics were a school of philosophers who believed that the good life was a life lived in accordance with nature, free from social conventions or restrictions. The Cynics (whose name comes from the Greek *kuôn*, meaning "dog") would demonstrate their rejection of conventional values by doing things in public that were considered disgraceful and by saying outrageous things to passersby.

The most famous Cynic was a philosopher called Diogenes, who was said to have lived in a barrel in the Athenian marketplace, where he scandalized the Athenians by neglecting his appearance and personal hygiene. If people weren't looking shocked enough, Diogenes would fall back on public masturbation—always guaranteed to cause a stir.

On one occasion, Alexander the Great was passing by Athens and came to see this notorious but much-admired thinker, who he found sunbathing happily. Was there, wondered the all-powerful king, any favor he could do for the esteemed Diogenes? The answer came: "Yes. You can stop blocking my light!"

In modern usage, the word cynic has lost its ideological aspect and simply means someone who is negative and rejects or disbelieves professed values.

CZAR

The Emperor of Russia; anyone given absolute authority in some sphere or department

The word Czar, used as a title of the emperors of Russia until the Revolution of 1917, is derived from the name of the great Roman general and dictator Julius Caesar who, for a brief period between 48 and 44 B.C., was the undisputed master of the Roman world.

Julius Caesar was assassinated in 44 B.C., but his reputation among the poor people of Rome remained stellar. So, when a his young relative, Octavian, became Rome's first emperor about a decade later, he did his best to present himself as the great dictator's natural successor. The ruler formerly known as Octavian would henceforth be called Augustus Caesar.

And each successive emperor after Augustus followed in his footsteps. All of them used the name Caesar as a way to emphasize their links to the original Julius Caesar, until the word stopped being a name and became a hereditary title. Even after the Roman Empire fell, European monarchs couldn't resist the glamour of the long-dead Julius. The word czar arrived in Russia via Gothic *Kaisar* and Old Slavic *Tsesari,* but essentially it's still the same ancient name.

D

DELPHIC RESPONSE

An answer which is ambiguous or obscure

For the ancient Greeks and Romans, oracles were important links between the human world and the world of the divine. It was believed that at special oracular shrines, scattered around Greece, the gods would use their knowledge of the future to answer the questions of ordinary mortals.

The greatest oracle of all was at the shrine of Pythian Apollo at Delphi. The sacred Pythian priestesses were blessed with the god's prophetic power, and even kings and tyrants would ask at Delphi before undertaking any important business. The important foreign policy decisions of the Greek states—whether to found a colony; whether to go to war—were all submitted for the approval of the Delphic Oracle.

Since they didn't actually know the future, the priests who provided the oracular answers had to be careful to cover their bases. King Croesus of Lydia famously asked at Delphi whether he should invade Persia. The Delphic response was that, if he invaded, he would destroy a great empire, so, full of optimism, Croesus marched off to attack the Persians. Within the year, his armies had been scattered and his once rich kingdom lay in ruins. But, of course, the Delphic Oracle wasn't wrong. After all, it told that a great empire would be destroyed—it just failed to mention that it would be his own.

GREAT ORACLES OF THE ANCIENT WORLD

The oracle at Delphi was not the only one in the ancient world. Other famous oracles include:

Epidaurus—Epidaurus was the site of a shrine to Asclepius, the god of medicine. Worshippers traveled here for answers to medical questions.

The Oracle of Trophonius at Lebedeia—Worshippers would go here and spend a night in a terrifying cave underground. Priests would then interpret their frightened babblings when they returned and provide an answer.

The Oracle of Zeus at Ammon—This Egyptian oracle was famously consulted by Alexander the Great before he destroyed the Persian Empire.

The Oracle of Zeus at Dodona—The oldest oracle in Greece, Zeus would answer questions here by rustling the sacred oaks, whose movements were interpreted by priestesses.

The Sibylline Books—A set of prophetic writings thought to have been acquired by the kings of Rome in the earliest years of Rome's history. They were consulted whenever the city was in trouble.

DEUS EX MACHINA

*The sudden intervention of some implausible event
to solve a seemingly impossible situation*

In ancient Greek theater, the *mêkhanê,* or "machine," was a crane that could lift actors above the stage as if they were flying. This early version of special effects was a lifesaver for dramatists who got their plots into a tangle and needed some divine intervention to straighten things out again.

The playwright Euripides was a particularly notorious user of the *mêkhanê*. In his play *Orestes,* a complex plot of kidnap and murder ends in a tense standoff between the Spartan king Menelaus and the eponymous hero. The stage is set for high drama, but the tension is immediately defused by the appearance of Apollo, who floats down on the crane, tells Menelaus to go home, sends Orestes to stand trial and marries everyone else to each other before being hoisted away back up to Olympus.

The phrase entered English by way of the Roman poet Horace, who identified the deus ex machina (or "god from the machine") as a cheap plot device that ought to be avoided. Sadly, judging by today's TV plotlines, Horace's criticism hasn't made much of a dent in the deus ex machina's enduring appeal.

DRACONIAN REGULATIONS

Exceptionally harsh laws or rules,
especially with severe punishments

Draco, whose name means "snake" or "dragon," was an Athenian aristocrat who lived during Greece's so-called Archaic Period in the seventh century B.C. He is remembered as the first person to give Athens a formal set of laws: the Draconian Code.

By giving society a formal set of written, binding rules, Draco took an important step forward along the road that would eventually produce Athenian democracy. Not that Draco's code was in any way a piece of wishy-washy liberalism. The penalty for most violations of the rules was death, or, for the very lucky, a life of slavery.

Draco's laws were too severe to last for long, and, within a few decades, they had been superseded by the more moderate reforms of Solon. Nevertheless, the harshness of Draco's legislation remains proverbial more than two and a half thousand years later.

DRINK FROM THE WATERS OF LETHE

To forget absolutely

In Greek and Roman mythology, the River Lethe ("oblivion" in Greek) was one of the five great rivers of the Underworld. Its waters were said to have the power to wash away memories. According to the beautiful (though unorthodox) account of the Underworld in Virgil's *Aeneid,* the souls of the dead were forced to drink from the River Lethe to erase the traces of their past lives before they could be born again in new bodies.

Today, people unconsciously invoke the spirit of Lethe when they achieve alcoholic oblivion by ordering a "lethal" cocktail.

THE FIVE RIVERS OF THE UNDERWORLD

Acheron—The river of sorrow on which the ferryman Charon plied his trade, carrying souls from the land of the living to the land of the dead

Cocytus—The river of lamentation

Lethe—The river of oblivion

Phlegethon—The river of flames

Styx—The river of hatred; oaths sworn by the River Styx were unbreakable even among the immortal gods

DULCE ET DECORUM EST PRO PATRIA MORI

"It is sweet and fitting to die for the fatherland"— often used ironically

This Latin phrase comes from one of the *Odes* of the Roman poet Horace, writing under the emperor Augustus. It was often quoted during the days of the British Empire, and served as a rousing reminder to young men of the attractions of a glorious death for one's country.

The phrase is now best known as the title of a poem written in 1917 by the war poet Wilfred Owen. In the poem, which describes the awful death of a soldier in a gas attack, the patriotic line becomes a cruel joke, the "old lie" that condemned a generation to slaughter.

> If in some smothering dreams you too could pace
> Behind the wagon that we flung him in,
> And watch the white eyes writhing in his face,
> His hanging face, like a devil's sick of sin;

If you could hear, at every jolt, the blood
Come gargling from the froth-corrupted lungs,
Obscene as cancer, bitter as the cud
Of vile, incurable sores on innocent tongues,—
My friend, you would not tell with such high zest
To children ardent for some desperate glory,
The old Lie: Dulce et decorum est
Pro patria mori.
— Wilfred Owen, *"Dulce et Decorum Est,"* 1917

What poor Horace would have thought of this use of his line is impossible to say. After living through the terrible civil war years, and a (somewhat inglorious) military career, Horace knew that war isn't all it's cracked up to be. But for a government-sponsored poet writing in the militaristic climate of ancient Rome, a certain amount of patriotic fervor was probably part of the job description.

E

ECHO

The repetition of sound due to the reflection of sound waves;
imitation or repetition of something already done

According to Ovid's *Metamorphoses,* Echo was the name of the nymph who was given the unenviable task of distracting the goddess Hera while her lecherous husband, Zeus, ran around the mountains trying to seduce the nymphs, dryads and other minor deities who lived there.

For a while, Echo was able to keep Hera distracted by telling her witty stories, but in the end, the goddess discovered that she was being tricked. In a rage, she put a curse on Echo that deprived her of her most prized asset: her eloquence. From that day on, Echo would only be able to repeat the words of others, never saying anything of her own.

In Ovid's version, Echo meets her end when she falls in love with cruel Narcissus, who loved only himself. Unable to declare her feelings for him because of Hera's curse, Echo wastes away until nothing is left but her voice, which haunts wild places and dark caves and can still be heard repeating the words of passersby.

ELECTRA COMPLEX

Wanting to kill your mother and marry your father;
the female equivalent of the Oedipus complex

Carl Jung proposed the term Electra complex in 1913 as a way of describing a supposed stage of female psychosexual development, during which girls would be sexually attracted to their fathers and jealous of their mothers.

The original Electra was a Mycenaean princess who played a central role in one of Greek mythology's bloodiest family breakdowns. Electra's father, Agamemnon, started the ball rolling when he sacrificed her sister Iphigenia to the gods before leaving for the Trojan War. But when Agamemnon returned from the war ten years later, his wife, Clytemnestra, with the help of her lover Aegisthus, cut him to pieces with a ceremonial axe.

With Clytemnestra and Aegisthus now producing babies of their own, Agamemnon's surviving children were always going to be in a rather tricky position. His son Orestes fled, while Electra was forcibly married to a local peasant to keep her from making trouble, or producing dangerous heirs. Furious, she spent every day praying to her beloved father's ghost for vengeance, which eventually came when Orestes returned from hiding. Together, the two siblings murdered Aegisthus and then their own mother.

EPIC

Very large or grand; dealing with big themes and ideas

Epic poetry is humanity's oldest literary genre—it was performed in Mesopotamia at the same time as the ancient Britons were erecting Stonehenge. In Greek, the first and greatest epics were

EPIC POETRY THROUGH THE AGES

c. 20th century B.C.	The Epic of Gilgamesh—Anonymous
8th century B.C.	Iliad and Odyssey—Homer
3rd century B.C.	Argonautica—Apollonius of Rhodes
1st century B.C.	The Aeneid—Virgil
c. 700s	Beowulf—Anonymous
1300s	Divine Comedy—Dante
1500s	The Faerie Queene—Spenser
1600s	Paradise Lost—Milton
1800s	Don Juan—Byron

the *Iliad* and the *Odyssey*, two long poems (at twenty-four books each), which told the story of the great Trojan War and of the hero Odysseus' dramatic voyage home.

The impact of these two poems on later Greek culture is hard to overstate. Their author, Homer, was regarded as an endless fountain of wisdom and poetic inspiration, a little like Shakespeare today. According to Plato, it was generally thought that Homer educated Greece and that you could arrange your whole life by this one poet.

Ancient readers would have been surprised to learn that many modern scholars now doubt that Homer existed at all. Current thinking is that the *Iliad* and the *Odyssey* are probably the work of many poets, who passed the ancient stories down and refined them over the generations.

But even the minor inconvenience of not actually existing couldn't stop Homer from becoming widely regarded as the greatest poet of all time. The imitations started early, and even two and a half thousand years later, poets such as John Milton could still be found building their own epic poems on the foundations Homer provided.

EROTICA

*Books, pictures or anything else designed
to stimulate sexual feeling*

In Greek mythology, Eros was the god of love, equivalent to the Roman Cupid, the familiar face of a million modern Valentine cards.

But the original Eros was a much more powerful and interesting figure than the cherubic Cupid with his bow and arrows. In the oldest Greek creation myths, Eros is born at the same time as Mother Earth, directly from the primordial Chaos. More elaborate tales have Eros hatching from the great World Egg, which was laid by Night, the first goddess. Either way, the Eros of these stories is a primitive and powerful force; at the cult center of Thespiae his statue was nothing more than a large phallic pole.

But this primitive vision was too crude for the sophisticated tastes of later Greeks. The basic urgings of sex were giving way to a more modern conception of love, and people needed a god to match. The poets of Hellenistic Alexandria were happy to oblige: Through generations of cutesy romantic verse, the mighty phallus-god of Greek creation was reduced to the chubby, unthreatening infant we know today.

ET TU, BRUTE?

An expression of reproach to a treacherous friend

In 44 B.C., the Roman general and dictator Julius Caesar, conqueror of Gaul and ruler of much of the known world, was murdered in broad daylight in the Theater of Pompey in Rome by a group of aristocratic conspirators. The assassins were led by Gaius Cassius Longinus and Marcus Junius Brutus, Caesar's close friend.

It was agreed upon that all of the sixty or so conspirators should strike a blow so all would share the guilt of the murder. As Caesar came into the theater, where the senate was due to meet, he found himself surrounded by a thicket of daggers, stabbing at his eyes and legs from all sides.

According to the Roman biographer Plutarch, Caesar struggled against his attackers until he saw his friend Brutus coming toward him, knife in hand. Shocked by this betrayal, Caesar sank to the ground, pulling his robe over his head in despair. Roman historians disagree about Caesar's last words, and even whether he said anything at all. However, the story that has passed into legend is that Caesar said: *"Et tu, Brute?"*—"Even you, Brutus?"—before he died.

EUREKA!

*I have it!; an exclamation marking the moment
of some discovery or brainwave*

The word eureka entered the English language through a story about the great Greek philosopher and mathematician Archimedes.

According to the story, Archimedes was searching for a way to measure the volume of irregularly shaped objects because King Hieron of Syracuse suspected his goldsmith of secretly adding base metals to his new gold wreath. The breakthrough came when Archimedes noticed that the level of his bathwater would rise when he stepped in and sink when he got out. The volume of the displaced water was exactly equal to the volume of whatever, or whoever, he put in the bath.

When this idea came to Archimedes, he exclaimed *"Heureka!"* (which, in ancient Greek, simply means "I've found it"), leaped from his bath and ran wildly around the streets of the city, dripping wet and stark naked. By putting the disputed wreath in a bucket of water, he could get an accurate measure of the wreath's volume, and therefore, an idea of how much it would weigh if it really was pure gold. Then, with a pair of ordinary scales, the dispute could be solved. Ever since, inventors and mathematicians who make discoveries have followed Archimedes in saying "Eureka!," although they've tended to keep their clothes on.

EUROPE

One of the world's seven continents

The continent of Europe is named after a Phoenician princess called Europa who, according to Greek mythology, was unfortunate enough to catch Zeus's attention while playing with her companions on the beach. Smitten with lust, Zeus took the form of a giant bull of extraordinary whiteness and beauty, and lay down in front of Europa on the sand.

Cautious at first, the princess eventually grew bolder, stroking the bull's magnificent hide before finally—and foolishly—climbing on its back. Immediately, the Zeus-bull took off, still carrying the now terrified girl, and sped straight across the sea to Crete where he could make his divine advances undisturbed.

Europa eventually bore Zeus three sons, the most famous of whom was Minos, the legendary founder of the Minoan civilization. Meanwhile her brother Cadmus, sent to look for her, ended up founding the city of Thebes on the Greek mainland. So, in mythology at least, Europa and her brother were at the very root of Greek, and therefore European, history.

F

FABLE

A short story intended to convey some moral message or wisdom

In the ancient world, fables, from the Latin *fabula*, meaning "story" (also the origin of the word fabulous), were a popular literary form in which some moral precept or proverb would be expressed with the help of a short narrative, often featuring animals, plants, mythical creatures, or forces of nature, which are given human qualities And these stories often take place in rustic, natural settings.

The most famous ancient composer of fables was a slave called Aesop, about whom little is known. He may have been originally a Thracian and probably lived during the sixth century B.C. What we do know is that by the fifth century B.C. his simple tales—or at least, tales attributed to him, such as "The Tortoise and the Hare" and "The Boy Who Cried Wolf"—were quoted across the Greek world. (See box page 70.) Many of them are still well-known today, and are the source of several modern phrases.

Fables have gone beyond well-known expressions, too, with appearances in modern adult fiction. George Orwell's *Animal Farm* satirizes Stalinist Communism in the form of an animal fable.

COMMON EXPRESSIONS FROM AESOP'S FABLES

The Boy Who Cried Wolf—a shepherd boy amuses himself by falsely claiming to have seen a wolf, in order to alarm some villagers. When a real wolf appears, the villagers ignore the boy, thinking that he is lying, and the wolf eats his flock.

The Dog in the Manger—a dog falls asleep in a manger, and when he wakes up, he spitefully prevents the oxen from eating the hay, although he has no use for it himself.

The Goose That Laid the Golden Eggs—a peasant has a magic goose that lays golden eggs. Thinking it must be made of gold inside, the peasant cuts open the goose and kills it.

The Lion's Share—a fox, a jackal and a lion go out hunting and catch a deer. However, when they divide the meat, the lion keeps it all for himself.

Sour Grapes—a hungry fox decides that a bunch of grapes that hangs just out of his reach is probably sour anyway.

The Tortoise and the Hare—a hare enters a race with a tortoise but is so confident that he takes a nap before reaching the finish line. The tortoise, who is slow and steady, overtakes him and wins the race.

The Wolf in Sheep's Clothing—a wolf disguises himself as a sheep, in order to steal a lamb to eat. But the shepherd, wanting some mutton for his supper, kills the wolf and eats him.

THE FACE THAT LAUNCHED A THOUSAND SHIPS

Helen of Troy

Was this the face that launch'd a thousand ships
And burned the topless towers of Ilium?
Sweet Helen, make me immortal with a kiss.

—Christopher Marlowe, *Dr. Faustus, c.* 1594, V.i.97-9

Marlowe's "Helen," whose face was so inspiring, is Helen of Troy, who is famous in Greek mythology as the most beautiful woman in the world. Her beauty was so extraordinary that by the time she was entering her teens, she had already been abducted once, by the lecherous Athenian hero Theseus.

To prevent this happening again, the assembled kings of Greece, who all hoped to have Helen for themselves, swore that they would defend Helen's future husband, whoever that person might be. Menelaus, king of Sparta, turned out to be the lucky man and the rival kings, bound by their oaths, returned disappointed to their homes.

When, some years later, poor Helen was abducted again by the Trojan prince Paris, the kings of Greece united to come to her rescue. Under the command of Agamemnon, high king in Mycenae, the huge armada (Marlowe's "thousand ships"), drawn from all corners of Greece, set sail for Troy to win Helen back.

FAITHFUL PENELOPE

A wife faithful to her husband even in the most trying circumstances

Penelope was the wife of the hero Odysseus, one of the many Greek kings who left their homes to join the great battle at Troy. But when the rest of the Greek heroes were coming back to their wives and families, Odysseus was nowhere to be found. And by the time ten years had passed, everyone except Penelope had given Odysseus up for dead.

Worse yet, all the local young men, attracted by her beauty, had arrived at Odysseus' palace and were refusing to leave until the supposed widow chose one of them to be her new husband. Penelope stalled these unwelcome suitors by telling them to wait until she'd finished weaving a burial shroud for Laertes, her aging father-in-law. She spent all day weaving ostentatiously but by night she would secretly unpick the day's work so that the shroud was never finished.

In the end, the long-awaited Odysseus did return to his Penelope. Entering the palace disguised as a beggar, he slaughtered all 108 suitors with his bow and arrows, and at last was reunited with his resourceful and faithful wife.

TO FALL ON ONE'S SWORD

*To commit suicide; of someone taking responsibility
for an error—to resign*

In the ancient world, suicide was widely regarded as a fairly honorable way to die. For public officials who failed in their duties or generals who were defeated in battle, suicide was routinely used as a way to win back some measure of lost pride.

Of course, in many cases, the only alternative to suicide was the shame of a public execution. Emperors such as Tiberius or Nero were famous for "inviting" people to commit suicide, an invitation that the unfortunate recipients knew better than to refuse. In Athens the philosopher Socrates was "allowed" to commit suicide (by drinking hemlock), when he was convicted of atheism and leading young men astray.

The preferred method among the Romans was to open the veins of the wrists while sitting in a hot bath. However, for those with a more theatrical bent who wished to go out in proper martial style, there was always the option of falling on one's sword. A running jump onto a sword that had been propped up on the ground was thought to be almost as glorious as a proper death in battle.

It doesn't seem so heroic when it's done like that.

WHAT THE FATES HAVE IN STORE

The future; destiny

The idea of the Fates can be found in many cultures, but the three Fate goddesses of ancient Greece may be the most famous contributors to our modern phrase.

In Greek the Fates were called the Moirae, and they were thought of as three sisters who would spin out the thread of a person's life and control their destiny. Clotho, the first sister, would create the thread, Lachesis would measure out each person's allotted length, while Atropos, the last sister, used her scissors to cut the thread when someone's life was at an end.

The Romans had a similar triad of goddesses, who they called the Parcae. Their statues in the Roman Forum were called the Fatae, which comes from *fatum*—"something that has been spoken"—and from which we get our modern word "fate."

TO FIDDLE WHILE ROME BURNS

To make merry while neglecting your responsibilities

Being a Roman emperor was no easy job. There were constant threats: mutinous legions, invading barbarians, and hidden assassins. It's probably not surprising, then, that some emperors did let the strain go to their heads. There was Domitian, who built his palace out of reflective moonstone, so he could see people coming up behind him; Caligula, who bestowed senatorial rank on his favorite horse; and Tiberius, who is supposed to have killed a man by rubbing him to death with a fish.

The most famous of the "bad" emperors was Nero, whose habit of using flaming Christians to brighten up his garden made him one of the world's earliest contenders for the title of Antichrist.

Like Hitler two thousand years later, Nero had delusions of artistic talent, and he liked to subject his courtiers to endless recitals of atrociously bad poetry, which he accompanied on the lyre. One aristocrat, Petronius, was overheard quoting Nero's verses about thunder while passing gas in a public toilet. He soon received a letter from the emperor "inviting" him to commit suicide.

74

But the most serious catastrophe of Nero's reign was the great fire of Rome in 64 B.C., for which he was generally, though unfairly, blamed. The historian Suetonius wrote that Nero had started the fire to gratify some insane urge, and that he watched its progress from a tower on the Esquiline Hill while singing and playing the lyre—hence the modern phrase "to fiddle while Rome burns."

FLORA AND FAUNA

Plants and animals

Flora and Fauna were two Roman goddesses whose names were adopted by the Swedish biologist Carl Linnaeus to represent the plant and animal kingdoms.

Before her unexpected promotion by an eighteenth-century Swede, Flora was a relatively minor goddess associated with flowers and springtime. It was Flora who made the trees blossom each year and who looked after all things in bloom. Her yearly festival, the Floralia, featured hares, goats, strippers, scatterings of beans and multicolored clothing, and she was a particular favorite among Rome's many prostitutes.

Fauna meanwhile was an even more obscure figure, a goddess of women, fertility and fortune-telling, who was the wife of the forest god Faunus. The "fauns" of later mythology (as used by C. S. Lewis in the Narnia series), with goat legs and horns, are all derived from Faunus, whose most famous festival, the Lupercalia, involved half-naked men hitting bystanders with bits of goat. It was, like the Floralia, surprisingly popular.

TO FLY TOO CLOSE TO THE SUN

*To get carried away by success and go beyond
the limits of your capabilities*

This phrase is an allusion to the escape of Daedalus and his son, Icarus, from the famous Cretan labyrinth.

Although the labyrinth was reputedly impossible to escape, Daedalus was no ordinary prisoner. Mythology's greatest craftsman, Daedalus had designed the labyrinth himself and was easily able to find a way out of his own maze. However, getting away from Crete was another matter, since King Minos, who had ordered their detention, controlled all available ships. In the end, Daedalus found the novel solution of building two pairs of full-sized wings, made of feathers and wax, and before long, he and his son were happily flying away from the island.

Unfortunately, the young Icarus soon became carried away with his new abilities and, ignoring his father's warnings, started flying closer and closer to the sun. Daedalus watched in horror as the wax holding Icarus' wings together melted under the sun's fiery heat, leaving the boy to plunge to his death in the sea down below. Since then, Icarus has been a powerful symbol of the dangers inherent in exuberance and success.

FORUM

*A public meeting or assembly for the exchange
of ideas and argument*

In the Roman world, every town had its forum. It was, first of all, a marketplace, an open area in the center of town where farmers and craftsmen could display their wares. But forums (or "fora" if you want to be really strict about it) were also at the center of civic life, providing the arena for religious ceremonies, legal trials and political battles.

As the world's capital, Rome naturally had to have the world's finest forum. In fact, Rome was so huge that it had several, but the oldest and most important was the *Forum Romanum,* or Roman Forum, the original heart of the city. Said to have been founded by Romulus himself, the Forum was full of legends and history. It had seen famous speeches and notorious trials, mob violence and murder, and in its busy chaotic splendor it held the essence of the city itself.

In later usage "forum" became a word for any public space or gathering devoted to discussion and the free exchange of ideas. The truest heirs to the rambunctious spirit of the original forums are now found online, where the same odd mixture of politics, argument, obscenity and mob violence reigns supreme.

G

THE GAIA HYPOTHESIS

A theory that the Earth is one self-regulating system and tends toward a healthy homeostatic state, as if it were a living organism

The Gaia hypothesis was developed in the 1960s by British scientist James Lovelock who argued that the planet Earth keeps itself stable and health, as if it were a vast living creature. When something disrupts the balance, argued Lovelock, there are living systems that pull the Earth back to a state of equilibrium.

If the world was going to be imagined as a sort of superbeing, she was going to need a name, and Lovelock settled on Gaia, after the Greek goddess Mother Earth. In the poet Hesiod's account of the creation of the universe, Gaia is the first being born out of the primordial Chaos. She is mother of the sky and the sea and of the Titans who ruled the heavens before the Olympian gods.

And, in a way, the mythological Gaia did try to keep regulating the world which she had created. The modern, scientific Gaia has to deal with the processes of biology and chemistry to keep things in order. The ancient Gaia, by contrast, was able to be more direct. When her husband Uranus (the Sky) was getting on her nerves, Gaia simply had her son Cronus cut off the offender's testicles with a magic sickle.

GLADIATORIAL ATMOSPHERE

A highly charged, belligerent atmosphere

Gladiatorial combat was the ultimate blood sport, an extraordinary form of entertainment that was extremely popular across the Roman Empire, until it was finally pushed out by Christianity in the fifth century A.D.

The earliest shows involved small numbers of slaves who would fight to the death in pairs to mark the funeral of some wealthy citizen. Before long, Republican politicians were putting on special gladiatorial shows, independent of funerals, as a way to gain instant favor with the general public.

By the Imperial period, games could last for days and involve thousands of gladiators, rather than the original two or three pairs. To accommodate these vast spectacles, the emperors built perhaps the most recognizable of all Roman monuments, the Colosseum. It was a marvel of ancient engineering in which the best gladiators from all over the empire would fight for the amusement of the 50,000-strong crowd.

Many would die (although most fights were not to the death) but some gladiators, despite being criminals or slaves, achieved huge celebrity. There were even whispers of scandalous affairs between gladiators and noblewomen. One gladiator from Pompeii was praised in local graffiti as "the one who makes girls sigh."

Certainly, for all the danger, gladiatorial combat in front of the roaring Colosseum crowd must have been the ultimate adrenaline rush. The football stadiums of modern times, often said to have "gladiatorial atmospheres" by optimistic journalists, would pale by comparison.

TYPES OF GLADIATOR

In ancient Rome, gladiators were divided into different classes, each with their own distinctive equipment and fighting techniques. Some of the most famous are:

Myrmillo—a heavily armed gladiator with a long shield, a sword and an armguard. Myrmillones wore odd-shaped helmets with fish emblems on the crest.

Retiarius—a lightly armored gladiator, armed with a net and a trident. Retiarii had to use superior mobility to trap their enemies for the killing blow.

Secutor—a heavily armed class of gladiator, specially adapted for fighting retiarii. Secutores had smooth round helmets, designed to escape entanglement in the retiarii's net.

Thraex—a gladiator in the "Thracian" style, armed with a small shield and a curved Thracian sword.

GOLDEN AGE

*An imagined time of perfect peace, virtue and prosperity;
the peak of something's existence or popularity*

According to the Greek poet Hesiod, the first humans were a "golden race" who lived in a state of bliss and didn't work or suffer through disease or war. Since then, said Hesiod, people have just been getting worse and worse by the year.

This idea quickly caught on with the Romans. The poet Ovid wrote about an Italian "golden age," when Saturn ruled the Earth and men knew nothing of commerce, ambition, agriculture or war. Perhaps, wrote Ovid optimistically, with the coming of the emperor Augustus, the golden age of men might return.

Not surprisingly, things didn't quite work out that way (and Ovid ended up being banished from Rome for writing rude verses). On the upside, each generation before and since then has had the comfort of being able to agree that "things aren't what they were in the good old days."

GORGON STARE

A look that could freeze blood

The three Gorgons, Sthenno, Euryale and Medusa, were famous monsters of Greek mythology. With boars' tusks, bronze hands and poisonous snakes for hair, they were so terrifying that anyone who looked them in the face would immediately turn to stone.

The only person to take on the Gorgons and live was the hero Perseus, son of Zeus and legendary founder of the city of Mycenae. Helped by his divine patron, Athena, he had the novel idea of attacking the Gorgons backward. Using the goddess's specially polished shield like a sort of ancient wing-mirror, he reversed toward the sleeping Medusa (the only mortal of the three), swiped off her head with a powerful backhand, and flew away, using winged sandals that he borrowed from the messenger god, Hermes.

Even in death, Medusa's hideous stare still had the power to turn people to stone, a fact that the cunning Perseus—who had taken the severed head with him—soon turned to his advantage. Before long, most of the hero's enemies were lifeless chunks of marble, including the giant Atlas, who became the Atlas mountain range. In the end, Perseus dedicated his gory trophy to Athena in gratitude for her help, and the goddess mounted it on her aegis where it could petrify (from the Greek *petros*, meaning "stone") her enemies ever after.

GOTH

Part of a modern subculture devoted to heavy-metal music and fond of dark clothing

Anyone who thinks that the "goths" of the modern world are scary should be glad that they don't have to meet the real thing. The original Goths were a more serious proposition than the troubled teenagers of today. They were a tribe of ferocious warriors, who originated in Scandinavia but slowly migrated south through the forests of Central Europe until, by the fourth century A.D., they were pressing at the Danube frontier of the Roman Empire.

In the 370s A.D., the Romans allowed the Goths (who were fleeing from the even scarier Huns behind them) to cross the border. But once they arrived they were treated terribly, until at last they revolted against Roman oppression. In 378 the Goths obliterated a Roman army at the battle of Adrianople and began to plunder the riches of the empire. Three decades later in 410, a Gothic army under Alaric finally sacked the imperial city of Rome.

GYMNASIUM

A place offering equipment, facilities and training for the promotion of physical fitness

The gymnasia of ancient Greece lay at the heart of Greek cultural life. Here young men would learn the skills that would enable them to be effective athletes, citizens and soldiers. Running, boxing and javelin throwing were all practiced, but gymnasia also became centers of learning and philosophical thought.

They were also central to the Greek tradition of pederasty, which encouraged older men to form romantic attachments to handsome youths. These relationships were thought to be an important part of a young man's education. The older *erastès*, or "lover," would give the young *erômenos*, or "beloved," the benefit of his experience and patronage; what these "lovers" would get in return is open to debate, but we can assume that they weren't all in it for the conversation.

For an old man looking for a young companion, a town's gymnasium was a sort of heaven of young athletic bodies and flexed muscles. Best of all (from a certain point of view), the only clothing allowed at these establishments was a thin coating of olive oil—in fact the very word gymnasium comes directly from the Greek *gymnos*, meaning "naked."

▣ H ▣

HALCYON DAYS

Times of happiness and prosperity

In Greek mythology, Alcyone was a daughter of Aeolus, the god of the winds. She was married to Ceyx, son of the Morning Star, and they enjoyed such a happy marriage that they claimed to be as lucky as the ultimate couple, Hera and Zeus.

This, of course, was a mistake. If there was one thing guaranteed to get the gods in a mood, it was hearing themselves being compared to lowly mortals. To punish Ceyx and Alcyone for their pride, Zeus changed them into birds: Ceyx became a diver, and Alcyone became a kingfisher, or *alkuon* in Greek.

Ovid has a different version of this story, where Alcyone is changed into a bird after her husband dies in a shipwreck. At any rate, both versions agree that the newly feathered Alcyone soon found a kingfisher's life to be far from straightforward. Every winter she would lay her eggs in a nest by the sea, and every year storms would sweep the nest away. Finally Zeus, taking pity on the unfortunate woman, decreed that for the seven days around the winter solstice the seas would always be calm. These tranquil days in the middle of winter are the halcyon days, which have come to stand for any period of peace and happiness.

HARPY

An unpleasant, angry, rapacious woman

The Harpies (whose name comes from the Greek word meaning "snatch") were early deities associated with stormy seas. With bird-like wings and legs but the faces and torsos of women, the Harpies delighted in causing trouble, carrying off children, or even souls, in their sharp claws.

The most famous legend in which the Harpies appear is the story of King Phineus, who they cruelly tormented. Every time a meal was spread out in front of the hungry king, the Harpies would appear and grab as much food as they could from the table before spewing out disgusting droppings over all the rest.

Despite being so unpleasant, the Harpies enjoyed a long afterlife in Western literature and art, cropping up in medieval paintings and heraldry and getting a cameo part in Dante's *Inferno* as monstrous guardians of people who have committed suicide. Ugly and greedy, the Harpies may be mythology's most repellent creatures. It's certainly a very rude name to call someone.

TO HECTOR

To browbeat or bully

In Homer's *Iliad,* the epic poem that tells the story of the Trojan War, the Trojan prince Hector appears as one of the most humane and admirable heroes involved in the fighting. His Greek counterpart Achilles is a godlike figure, terrifying in battle and full of blazing passions. Hector, by contrast, is a capable warrior and general but also a loving family man. In one of the *Iliad*'s most moving scenes, Hector, alone with his family during a break in the fighting, realizes that his shining helmet is terrifying his baby son and symbolically removes it to show the human face underneath.

Against the relentless force of Achilles' anger, Hector has no chance. In a final humiliating battle, Achilles chases Hector around the walls of Troy, kills him and insults his body by dragging it behind his chariot like a piece of meat. With Hector dead Troy is doomed to fall, and the *Iliad* closes with Hector's funeral.

As a final indignity for this unfortunate Trojan, early modern European playwrights inexplicably cast him as a thuggish bully, giving rise to his name's unflattering modern usage.

> All Troy then moves to Priam's court again,
> A solemn, silent, melancholy train:
> Assembled there, from pious toil they rest,
> And sadly shared the last sepulchral feast.
> Such honors Ilion to her hero paid,
> And peaceful slept the mighty Hector's shade
>
> Homer, *Iliad,* trans. Alexander Pope, bk. xxiv

HEDONISM

Devotion to sensual pleasure

Epicurus is one of the most misunderstood ancient Greek philosophers. Out of his whole philosophy, the part that has stuck in modern consciousness is his concept of hedonism: the idea that the only point of life is to pursue pleasure, or *hêdonê* in Greek.

To later interpreters this idea conjured visions of debauched feasts and orgies and all sorts of ancient Greek misbehavior, and the result is that in modern usage, "hedonism" is usually something that doesn't win approval.

But the "pleasure" that Epicurus regarded as life's ultimate goal was not the sensuous, bodily sort of pleasure that critics imagined. What Epicurus meant by "pleasure" was a profound mental state of balance and freedom from fear. The original hedonistic lifestyle was a calm, moderate and philosophical existence, lived in self-sufficiency and seclusion in the company of friends and loved ones.

What distinguished the Epicurean pursuit of pleasure from other philosophies was that for Epicurus, there was no divine reward waiting for virtue, and no transcendent spiritual truth to be sought after. Instead he taught that humans are nothing but atoms and that our souls, as well as our bodies, disappear when we die and leave nothing behind. His teachings inspired the following epitaph, found on tombstones across the Roman Empire, and still used today: "I was not; I have been; I am not; I do not mind."

HERCULEAN TASK

An impossible or extremely difficult job

Hercules, or Heracles as he was known to the Greeks, was the greatest hero of classical mythology. He was a son of Zeus, who took so long to beget him, as it were, that the great god had to slow down the moon and the sun and stretch one night into three.

By the time Heracles was an adult, he was acknowledged to be by far the strongest hero of his time. Unfortunately, Zeus's wife, Hera, was not too fond of this product of her husband's adulterous coupling, so one night the jealous goddess caused Heracles to go temporarily insane and kill his own wife and children.

In penance for this terrible murder, Heracles was forced to carry out twelve labors, set for him by his detested cousin Eurystheus.

This lanky king was so unheroic that when, for one labor, Heracles succeeded in bringing home the terrifying Erymanthian Boar, he jumped into a giant clay pot where he hid, whimpering, until the coast was clear.

Heracles' twelve labors took him to the outer limits of the known world at the time. They had him fight monsters that should have been invincible, including a lion whose skin was impenetrable; some man-eating horses; and even Cerberus himself, the terrifying three-headed dog who was believed to guard the gates of the Underworld. A Herculean task has since become shorthand for any impossibly difficult undertaking.

THE TWELVE LABORS OF HERACLES

1. To kill the Nemean Lion
2. To kill the Hydra of Lerna
3. To capture the Erymanthian Boar
4. To capture the Cerynaean Hind
5. To destroy the Stymphalian Birds
6. To clean the stables of Augeas
7. To retrieve the Cretan Bull
8. To fetch the man-eating mares of Diomedes
9. To steal the girdle of the Amazon queen Hippolyta
10. To rustle the cattle of Geryon
11. To bring back Cerberus from the Underworld
12. To take one of the apples of the Hesperides from their garden at the end of the world

HERMAPHRODITE

*Someone with both male and female sexual characteristics
or organs*

The demigod Hermaphroditus, named after his parents Hermes
and Aphrodite, started life as an ordinary—and a very handsome—man. One hot summer day, the story goes, while swimming
in a lake, he caught the attention of one of the water nymphs called
Salmacis.

Swept away with desire, Salmacis threw herself on the unfortunate young man, winding her limbs with his and praying all the
while to the Olympian gods that she and Hermaphroditus should
never be separated. As she clung to him, the immortals fulfilled her
wish. She and Hermaphroditus were fused together in one body, at
once both male and female.

Hermaphroditus was only the first of many sexually ambiguous
characters in Greek mythology. The Theban prophet Tiresias, for
example, was born a man but spent some years living as a woman.
It was he who settled an argument among the gods about whether
men or women received greater pleasure from the act of sex, saying
(in Robert Graves's formulation):

> If the parts of pleasure be numbered ten
> Nine parts go to women, and one to men.
> > Pseudo-Apollodorus, *Bibliotheca,* III.vi.7

HIPPOCRATIC OATH

*A solemn promise made by doctors to always
uphold medical ethics*

Hippocrates of Kos was a legendary figure who was thought to be the founding father of Greek medicine. According to ancient biographers, Hippocrates traveled across the ancient world performing marvelous feats of healing and teaching numerous disciples as he moved along. He was also said to be the author of the Hippocratic Corpus, a collection of medical texts, which had the last word in ancient medical science.

The Hippocratic Corpus, which still survives today, was probably written by several authors rather than by one extraordinary man. Even so, the collection is a fascinating record of the way medicine developed as a science in the ancient world. In addition to giving practical advice for the treatment of various illnesses, the Hippocratic Corpus also contains one of the world's earliest statements of medical ethics: the Hippocratic Oath.

These days some of the terms of the oath (for example, making doctors swear not to seduce any of their patients' slaves) can seem out of date. Nevertheless, the essential tenets of modern medical ethics—do no harm, medical confidentiality, and don't kill your patients—are all there in the Hippocratic Oath which is, in modified form, still taken by doctors to this day.

HOI POLLOI

The masses; ordinary people

In ancient Greek, *hoi polloi* simply means "the many," used in a political sense to mean the ordinary people. The *polloi* were the opposite of the *oligoi,* meaning the aristocratic "few" (as in "oligarch"). To the democratic Athenians, being called one of the *polloi* was generally a compliment, but grand Englishmen during the modern era rediscovered the phrase "hoi polloi" as a snooty way of dismissing the lower classes. Not only was it rude, it had the bonus appeal of being incomprehensible to the people it was meant to insult, who were sadly deprived of a proper classical education.

TO BE LIKE HORATIUS AT THE BRIDGE

To stubbornly defy overwhelming odds

For the first two and a half centuries of its existence, Rome was ruled by a line of kings. Around 509 b.c. the last of these kings, Tarquinius Superbus ("Tarquin the Proud"), was overthrown by disgruntled aristocrats, and the Romans set up their famous Republican system.

But Tarquin and his sons refused to accept defeat. Four years after they had been overthrown, they returned with an army of Etruscan soldiers and smashed Roman forces on the west bank of the River Tiber. Soon they were advancing toward the city itself, which lay on the far side of the river, connected by a single wooden bridge.

According to Roman tradition, the city was saved by the courage of Horatius Cocles. With two companions, Horatius earned his place in Roman legend by holding off the entire Etruscan army—three men standing against a horde until the retreating Romans were able to cut the Tiber bridge behind them and secure the city. When the bridge finally fell, Horatius is said to have plunged, fully armored, into the river, which carried him safely across to the other side, where he became one of Rome's great national heroes.

> Then out spake brave Horatius,
>   The Captain of the gate:
> 'To every man upon this earth
>   Death cometh soon or late.
> And how can man die better
>   Than facing fearful odds,
> For the ashes of his fathers,
>   And the temples of his Gods, ...'
>   —from Thomas Babington Macaulay, *Horatius*

ACT OF HUBRIS

A proud or arrogant thing to do

"Hubris" was a central concept in Greek society and mythology. The word has no direct translation in English, but it can be loosely defined as proud, violent and abusive behavior. In Athenian law, the term was generally used for acts that involved humiliation or dishonor to the victim. To strike a man in the face might be hubris. To insult the gods would certainly be hubris—a very foolish type of hubris.

Greek mythology and literature are full of examples of hubris meeting its divine punishment, or "nemesis." Over and over again, the pattern repeats: mortal gets good at something; feels pleased with him or herself; insults gods by claiming to be their equal; all comes to a sticky end. And punishment was never what we in the modern world might call proportionate. The satyr Marsyas was flayed alive just for daring to challenge Apollo to a music competition.

In modern usage, hubris has lost its connotation of violence and is used simply as a word for pride or arrogance.

HYDRA-HEADED

*Something that's dangerous, has many branches
and gets stronger the more it's attacked.*

The second of the hero Heracles' famous twelve labors was to kill the Hydra of Lerna, a horrifying swamp-dwelling creature with a doglike body and an array of hissing serpent heads, which spewed out poisonous breath.

Greece's greatest hero, Heracles was very capable of holding his breath long enough to avoid these poisonous fumes. However, even he must have been somewhat disconcerted by the monster's next trick: Every time he struck off one of its many heads, the Hydra would sprout two more heads in its place.

In the end, Heracles was only able to dispatch the Hydra with the help of his nephew and charioteer, a young man named Iolaus, who stood by with a burning torch. Each time Heracles chopped off a head, Iolaus would leap in and cauterize the wound to prevent more heads from growing back.

At last, the Hydra was defeated. Its many necks ended in burned stumps, and its final, central head, which was immortal and made of gold, had been chopped off and buried under a rock.

I

I CAME. I SAW. I CONQUERED.

An expression of self-congratulation on the occasion of some success

According to the Roman historian Suetonius, these words were used by the great Roman general Julius Caesar to announce his victory in 47 B.C. over King Pharnaces II of Pontus, in modern Turkey. The Pontic king had rebelled against Roman authority and managed to defeat the small Roman force that was initially sent against him.

If this modest victory made Pharnaces feel smug, the feeling probably vanished pretty fast when Julius Caesar advanced into Pontic territory at high speed and crushed the rebel army with almost dismissive ease. To describe his victory, Caesar said only, "Veni. Vidi. Vici." Which means, in English, "I came. I saw. I conquered."

J

JANUS-FACED

Two-faced; hypocritical

Janus was a Roman god with a very distinctive feature: He had two faces—one on the front of his head, which gazed into the future, and one on the back, which looked into the past.

Aside from being rather odd-looking, Janus had a vague and ambiguous set of religious roles. He was associated with doors, prophecy and beginnings and endings, and his temple had a mysterious association with war that even the Romans didn't fully understand. The long-standing tradition was that the gates to his temple could only be shut when Rome was at peace (something that happened only a handful of times in Roman history). Janus was also credited with spending a period of time ruling on Earth, in Latium—the area around Rome.

Unlike most Roman gods, Janus has no Greek counterpart. He seems to be an entirely Italian creation, and historians have conjectured that Janus was one of the earliest gods of Roman religion—perhaps the supreme god of an archaic pantheon that existed before the arrival of later Greek influences.

BY JOVE

A polite but old-fashioned exclamation of surprise

Like "gadzooks," "By Jove" was used historically as a polite way to avoid saying "By God," which would have been considered blasphemous. Jove was an archaic English name for the Roman god Jupiter, equivalent to the Greek god Zeus. Like Zeus, Jupiter was the chief of all the gods, a god of the sky, storms and lightning. His temple of Jupiter Optimus Maximus (Jupiter the Best and Greatest) had a proud place on Rome's Capitoline Hill, the symbolic heart of the ancient city.

Jove is also the source of the word jovial—not that Jupiter was an easygoing, cheery sort of god. Although sometimes benevolent, he was generally a stern ruler with a tendency to throw thunderbolts when angry. In fact, jovial comes from the planet Jupiter, named after the Roman god, which, according to traditional astrology, makes those born under its sign cheerful, sanguine and outgoing.

L

LABYRINTH

A complicated network of passages or paths; a maze

The original labyrinth was built by the legendary craftsman Daedalus on the orders of King Minos of Crete. It was a maze so complicated and tangled that once in, no one could ever find their way out.

Minos's motivation for this bizarre construction project was an embarrassing family secret. His wife, Pasiphaë, had been cursed by Aphrodite to fall in love with a bull and soon after she produced a monstrous baby, with a human body but a bull's head. Unwilling to kill this creature who was, after all, a member of the family, Minos had him locked away in the labyrinth, never to emerge again.

To keep this "Minotaur" fed, Minos arranged that every year the city of Athens would send him a tribute of seven young men and seven young women who would be locked in the labyrinth to be devoured by the monster. This cruel practice was ended by the Athenian hero Theseus. He was given a ball of string by Minos's daughter Ariadne and saved himself from getting lost by unwinding it behind him as he traveled to the heart of the maze. After confronting and killing the Minotaur, the hero was able to follow the thread back to the exit and make his escape.

LOTUS EATER

*A person given to indolent enjoyment; someone who has
abandoned duty in the pursuit of pleasure*

The Lotus Eaters were a tribe in Greek mythology who lived off the
North African coast and survived by eating the fruit of the lotus
plant, which was said to be supernaturally delicious.

The hero Odysseus famously encountered the Lotus Eaters on his
way home from Troy when some of his scouts, exploring an unknown
island, were offered the lotus by its inhabitants. As soon as it passed
their lips, they forgot all thoughts of home or of their mission, and
they had no desire other than to eat more of the enchanted fruit.

Odysseus, who found them munching away several hours later,
took a tough-love approach to his intoxicated sailors, dragging them
back weeping to the ships and sailing away as fast as he could. Since
then, the Lotus Eaters have been a symbol for the temptations of
pleasure over duty—perhaps literature's first recorded drug addicts.

LUCULLAN FEAST

A particularly sumptuous or extravagant meal

Lucius Licinius Lucullus (*c.* 114–57 B.C.) was a Roman general who lived at the end of the Republican period of Rome's history. He was an outstanding military leader, achieving a string of remarkable victories against the odds and pushing out the frontiers of Roman rule as far as the Caucasus Mountains. However, for all his skill on the battlefield, Lucullus clearly wasn't much of a politician. Just as he was tying up the loose ends of his eastern campaign, his great rival, Pompey, arrived and stole most of the credit for his hard work.

Robbed of his glory, Lucullus returned to Rome but refused to reenter political life. Instead he devoted himself to extravagance on a scale that shocked his contemporaries, spending vast sums on gardens and libraries, and even more on hi-tech fish farms, which were ruinously expensive. An ill-advised attempt to breed birds in his dining room was abandoned because of the droppings, but in all other respects Lucullus turned out to be just as good at producing a twenty-course banquet as he had been at chopping the heads off unruly Armenians. His name became a byword for expensive living.

LYSISTRATA STRATEGY

To withhold sex in an effort to gain political leverage

Lysistrata is a character in an ancient Athenian comedy who famously ends the Peloponnesian War by encouraging the women of Greece to go on a sex strike. With a band of women from Athens and from the enemy city of Sparta, Lysistrata locks herself up on the Acropolis and announces that there will be no more sex for anybody until the fighting stops.

This extraordinary scenario gives the playwright Aristophanes plenty of scope for a string of outrageous jokes, and there was nothing the ancient comedians liked better than a good honest pun about genitals or bodily functions. Even so, the play bears a serious message about the terrible madness of war. "After all," Athenian audiences might have thought, "if even women can see this is a stupid battle to be fighting, why can't we?"

Although the Lysistrata strategy sounds a bit implausible—and certainly could never have really happened in the highly sexist society of ancient Greece—there have been modern sex strikes. Most famously, the Colombian "strike of the crossed legs" in 2006 saw wives of gang members refusing sex in an effort to get their husbands to surrender their guns.

TO BE A MAECENAS

To be a patron of the arts

The Roman emperor Augustus (63 B.C.–A.D. 14) was helped in his rise to power by two highly capable and very different friends. On the one hand was his general, Marcus Vipsanius Agrippa, an extremely competent fighter and strategist who became a sort of defense minister under the Augustan regime. On the other hand was Maecenas, a nobleman of Etruscan origin who became an unofficial minister of culture and the world's greatest patron of the arts.

By supporting such distinguished poets as Virgil, Horace and Propertius, Maecenas helped produce one of the world's greatest periods of artistic creativity. The works that he sponsored are still remembered two millennia later, and his name has become synonymous with benevolent artistic patronage.

Like many sponsors of art, Maecenas did occasionally venture to produce some verses of his own. It's a testament to the unchanging and eternal nature of artistic snobbery that all Maecenas's generosity couldn't buy him a good review; ancient critics snootily dismissed his poetry as having an affected style.

TO RUN A MARATHON

To take part in one of the world's many "marathon" races, always over a course of 26 miles and 385 yards

In 490 B.C. a small army of Athenians and their allies defeated the all-powerful Persian king Darius I on the plains of Marathon, about 26 miles from Athens. It was a pivotal moment in Western history. Darius was master of most of the known world, and his vast armies had been unstoppable. But the outnumbered Greek hoplites (heavy infantry), fighting in their unique battle formation, the phalanx, had stopped him dead in his tracks. Greece would remain independent, and the turmoil of her chaotic city-states would be the crucible for many of the ideas that underpin Western culture today.

Unsurprisingly, given the importance of the battle, it soon grew its own body of associated myths and legends. Soldiers reported seeing the gods Heracles and Pan fighting on the Greek side, just as British troops claimed to have seen angels in the fighting at Mons, two and a half thousand years later. The most famous story is one of a messenger called Pheidippides, who was sent back to Athens to bring the news of the victory. In his excitement, he ran the 26 miles back to the city, gasped "we've won," and then promptly dropped dead of exhaustion.

The modern marathon race was developed when the Olympic Games were being reinstituted at the end of the nineteenth century, and it commemorates Pheidippides' legendary run.

MARTIAL SPIRIT

Fighting spirit or military temperament

The word martial comes from the name of Mars, the Roman god of war. Although he was later thought to be the same as the Greek god Ares, Mars had a much more important religious role than his Greek counterpart.

The warlike Romans were particularly fond of Mars, and they claimed him as their main divine ancestor. The legend was that Mars made love to a mortal girl, Rhea Silvia. She eventually bore him two children, Romulus and Remus, who were suckled by a she-wolf. Romulus, after killing his brother in a quarrel, went on to found the city of Rome, which is named after him.

MAUSOLEUM

An exceptionally magnificent tomb

Mausolus was a ruler of Caria in ancient Turkey from 377 to 353 B.C., who is best known not for how he lived, but for the tomb in which he was buried after he died. This tomb, named the Mausoleum after its intended occupant, was constructed out of the finest materials by the finest artists in the Greek world. Standing high over the city of Halicarnassus, the Mausoleum lasted for more than one and a half thousand years before finally being broken up by the Knights of St. John, who used its marble to fortify their castle walls.

MENTOR

A wise adviser or senior supporter

Mentor is the name of a minor character in Homer's *Odyssey,* an aged nobleman on the island of Ithaca, who acted as an adviser to Prince Telemachus while the king, Odysseus, was away fighting at Troy.

Although his name has become proverbial, Mentor himself only deserves limited credit for good advice. In fact, the most famous "Mentor" speeches were delivered by the goddess Athena, who used Mentor's human form as a convenient disguise when she wanted to come and interfere with the action. Homer doesn't record what became of the real Mentor while Athena was impersonating him, but he probably spent most of the *Odyssey* snoring away happily in a divinely induced slumber.

MEPHITIC SWAMP

A sulphurous, stinking marsh; metaphorically
a den of corruption or vice

Ancient Roman religion was always a mixed bag. On the one hand were the grand gods who were worshipped on the Capitol and in the city's greatest temples. These lofty divinities were closely linked with their Greek counterparts: Jupiter was Zeus; Juno was Hera; and Venus was Aphrodite.

But beyond the rich temples of these Olympian deities there was another, older set of purely Italian gods, who played a more humble but important role in Roman life. Pomona, the goddess of orchards, was patron of the fruit growers. Consus was god of granaries. Sterculius was god of manure. There was even a Robigus, the god of mildew.

One of the most famous was Mephitis, the goddess of bad smells, whose modest temples could be found all over Italy, especially around the sulphurous volcanic vents of Mount Vesuvius. Unlike most of her fellows, Mephitis has had the dubious good fortune of becoming proverbial in the English language for anything with a foul and rotten stench. She also lent her name to two animal species: the hooded skunk (*Mephitis macroura*) and its cousin, the striped skunk (*Mephitis mephitis*).

MERCURIAL

Lighthearted, changeable, unstable

The word mercurial originally referred to people born under the sign of the planet Mercury, named after the Roman god of the same name. In the Roman Pantheon, Mercury was the protector of traders and commerce (his name comes from the same root as the word merchant) and the messenger of the gods. Mercury was a god of speed and cunning rather than straightforward majesty and strength. So it's appropriate that he gave his name to the hottest and smallest of the planets, as well as to a metal that's famous for remaining fluid and changeable even at room temperature.

MIDAS TOUCH

The ability to achieve easy wealth or success in any endeavor

Midas was a mythical king of Phrygia in modern Turkey, who was the hero of several popular Greek legends. The most famous comes from the *Metamorphoses* by the Roman poet Ovid.

Midas, the story goes, once helped the old satyr Silenus, who had passed out drunk in the Phrygian mountains. In gratitude, Silenus's master Dionysus granted the king one wish of his choosing, whatever it might be. The foolish Midas, letting greed cloud his judgement, prayed to the god that anything he touched might turn to gold.

For a while, this power was probably a lot of fun, but certain crucial drawbacks soon became apparent. As he sat down to a magnificent feast in his by now very shiny palace, he found to his horror that his food turned to gold as soon as it touched his lips. His fine imported wines just clanked uselessly against his teeth. In one version he even accidentally transformed his own daughter.

Luckily for Midas, Dionysus was kind enough to cure him of his terrible gift by washing him in the River Pactolus, which was famously full of gold ore forever afterward. The lesson, of course, was that there's more to life than making money, but oddly, in modern usage, the phrase has lost its cautionary meaning. These days, having the Midas touch is regarded as a good thing.

MONEY

Currency; a medium of value that can be traded for goods or services

Many words in English can be traced back to a Latin root. However, the story of the word money is rather more complicated than most, reaching all the way back into the depths of Roman mythology. It starts with the invasion of Rome by barbarian Gauls, who sacked the city. The remaining defenders shut themselves in the citadel on the Capitoline Hill, locked the gates, and hoped the Gauls would go away.

But the Gauls had other ideas. Climbing up the crags that surrounded the supposedly impregnable fortress, the Gaulish warriors were on the point of slipping over the walls when they were noticed by a gaggle of geese that lived on the Capitol and were sacred to the goddess Juno. The geese started honking so loudly that they woke the sleeping defenders who, led by the fantastically named Marcus Manlius, managed to repulse the attacking raiders.

Forever afterward, according to ancient theories, Juno was known as Juno Moneta, meaning "Juno Who Warns." When, years later, the Roman mint was established in the Temple of Juno Moneta, the epithet came to be associated with all things financial and became the root of our modern word money.

TO BE SOMEBODY'S MUSE

To be the source of someone's inspiration

The Muses were a group of goddesses who were the divine sources of art and culture, associated with Apollo and Dionysus, and broadly worshipped in ancient Greece.

Classical poets conventionally regarded themselves as vessels to be filled by the Muses' divine inspiration. Ancient poems often open by inviting some Muse to use the poet as a mouthpiece: "Sing, goddess, of the anger of Achilles, son of Peleus" is the famous first line of Homer's *Iliad*. Likewise, in the *Aeneid*, Virgil asks the Muse to tell the story through him.

> O Muse! the causes and the crimes relate;
> What goddess was provok'd, and whence her hate;
> For what offence the Queen of Heav'n began
> To persecute so brave, so just a man;
> —Virgil, *Aeneid*, i.11-14, trans. John Dryden

The Muses remained popular figures in poetry and art throughout the Middle Ages and the Renaissance. Invocations to the Muse can be found in Dante and Chaucer, and even John Milton, a stern Christian, invoked the pagan Muse at the beginning of his epic *Paradise Lost*.

In today's more secular world, the Muses have been mostly forgotten. Modern poets generally take the credit for their work themselves rather than claiming to have been possessed by three-thousand-year-old deities. Nevertheless, in words like music and museum, the memory of the Muses lives on.

THE NINE MUSES

Although ancient sources vary widely on how many Muses there were, and on their names and functions, a list of nine has become traditional:

Calliope—epic poetry	**Polyhymnia**—mime
Clio—history	**Terpsichore**—light verse and dance
Erato—lyric poetry	**Thalia**—comedy
Euterpe—flute-playing	**Urania**—astronomy
Melpomene—tragedy	

N

NARCISSIST

*Someone who is exceptionally vain
and pleased with him or herself*

There are various versions of the Narcissus story, but all the sources agree that he was a young man of superlative beauty. All through his life, men and women were constantly falling in love with him, but he scornfully rejected all their advances. In one account of the myth, he even sent an overeager suitor a sword with which to kill himself.

Narcissus finally found love when, out on a hunting trip, he bent down to drink from a forest pool and caught sight of his own reflection in the dark water. Immediately, he was captivated by the beauty he saw before him. Finally, in this mysterious water-dwelling youth, he had found someone worthy of his affections. Narcissus waved, the youth waved back. Narcissus leaned in for a kiss and the youth welcomingly pouted up at him. But when their lips should have touched, Narcissus found himself in the water, and the beautiful image was gone.

Infatuated and unfulfilled, Narcissus remained by the water gazing stupidly at his reflection until finally, hunger and cold ended his sufferings. The flowers that sprang up at the spot where he died still bear his name today.

NECTAR AND AMBROSIA

Particularly delicious food or drink

In Greek mythology, ambrosia and nectar were the food and drink of the gods. According to Homer, ambrosia was the food while nectar was the drink, but both substances were very mysterious, with properties and natures that vary widely from one version to the next.

We can at least be sure that nectar and ambrosia provided much more than simple nourishment. In the *Odyssey,* ambrosia is used at one point as an ancient beauty treatment: One dose for Odysseus's wife, Penelope, makes her look ten years younger. In another legend, ambrosia gives Achilles his famous power of invulnerability. Aphrodite is said to have used the divine food as a perfume, while on a couple of occasions it served as a preservative for corpses.

Modern scholars have advanced several theories about what nectar and ambrosia might have been. Most famously, Robert Graves and others have suggested that ambrosia was a name for a sacred species of "magic mushroom," which would certainly explain some of Greek mythology's more bizarre stories.

NEMESIS

The cause of someone's downfall

"Nemesis" was the name of the Greek goddess of vengeance, the implacable bringer of divine punishment who specialized in humbling the proud and destroying those who offended the gods.

As a goddess, Nemesis was said to be a daughter of Nyx (Night) and a sister to gods, including Hypnos (Sleep) and Thanatos (Death), but like her siblings, Nemesis was as much an abstract concept as a traditional deity. Specifically she represented the idea that pride, or hubris as the Greeks called it, really does come before a fall.

When the Persians invaded Greece with a vast force in the fifth century B.C., they were so confident of success that they had already bought the block of marble for their victory monument. When the outnumbered Greeks astonished the world by crushing the Persian army at the battle of Marathon, they carved the captured marble into a statue of Nemesis, which became the centerpiece of the goddess's most important shrine.

NYMPHOMANIA

A female addiction to sexual intercourse

In Greek mythology, the nymphs were the hundreds of minor goddesses who presided over each tree, stream, mountain or lake of the Greek landscape. As their name (from the Greek *numphê*, or "bride") suggests, the nymphs represented the fertility and beauty of the natural world.

During the 1700s the word nymphomania entered English vocabulary to describe a supposed female condition of uncontrollable sexual desire. For the poor nymphs, this hijacking of their good name is truly undeserved. In mythology, the nymphs seemed to spend all their time fending off the unwanted advances of horny satyrs and lustful Olympians—certainly not the other way around.

THE NYMPHS

Greek mythology has several kinds of nymph associated with different natural features. The main types are:

Alseids—nymphs of sacred groves

Dryads—the nymphs of trees

Hesperides—the nymphs of the evening; famous for their garden, in which grew a tree that produced golden apples

Hyades—rain nymphs, constantly grieving for their brother Hyas

Meliads—nymphs associated with ash trees

Naiads—the nymphs of rivers, springs and streams

Nereids—the nymphs of calm seas; daughters of Nereus

Oceanids—water nymphs; daughters of Oceanus and Tethys

Oreads—nymphs of the mountains

Pleiades—seven nymphs associated with Artemis; later transformed into a constellation

OCEAN

A large body of water or liquid

According to the early geography of the ancient Greeks, the world was a flat disk, with Greece and the Mediterranean at its center.

THE SEAS OF GREECE

The ancient Greeks were avid sailors who depended on the sea for food, travel and trade. The seas around Greece had names that tied them into the fabric of Greek mythology.

The Aegean Sea—named after Aegeus, the father of Theseus. Aegeus mistakenly thought that his son had been killed by the monstrous Minotaur and threw himself into the sea.

The Hellespont—a pair of twins, Helle and Phrixus, escaped from their cruel stepmother on the back of a flying ram. On the way, Helle slipped off and fell into the sea, which still bears her name.

The Icarian Sea—named after Icarus, who drowned in this sea after flying too close to the sun with his artificial wings.

The Ionian Sea—named after the nymph Io, who was beloved by Zeus but was transformed into a cow and driven around the Ionian Sea by a gadfly, sent by the jealous goddess Hera.

O

The very farthest edge of the Earth was thought by the Greeks to be marked by a great river, which they called Oceanus. In mythological terms, Oceanus was said to be the eldest son of Uranus (sky) and Gaia (Earth) and to be the father of all other rivers, including the famous rivers of the Underworld.

Medieval geographers, only aware of the land masses of Eurasia and Africa, named the body of water that encircled the two continents *Mare Oceanum* (the Ocean Sea) after the Greek deity, which in turn gave rise to the word's modern usage.

TO GO ON AN ODYSSEY

To go on a long and arduous journey or mission

The *Odyssey* is an epic poem about the adventures of the legendary Greek hero Odysseus on his return from the Trojan War. After ten years besieging the city, the unlucky hero spent ten more years wandering the farthest edges of the world before he finally returned to Ithaca, his island home.

During his journey, Odysseus would see most of his men eaten by cannibals, nearly be murdered by a one-eyed giant, narrowly avoid being transformed into a pig, offer a blood sacrifice in the land of the dead, and end up shipwrecked and stranded, by now the only survivor of his entire crew, on an island with an amorously inflamed (and highly possessive) goddess called Calypso.

His progress certainly wasn't helped by the fact that he had managed to accidentally kill one of the sons of the god Poseidon. Given that the only way for Odysseus to get home was by sea, and that Poseidon was a sea god, this proved to be somewhat problematic. When the Phaeacians (a mythical nation of seafarers) eventually lent Odysseus a ship for the last leg of his journey, Poseidon was so angry that he turned the vessel to stone right in the middle of Phaeacia's harbor to serve as a visible, and very inconvenient, reminder of his wrath.

OEDIPUS COMPLEX

Subconscious feelings in a man of jealousy toward his father, and sexual attraction toward his mother; the opposite of an Electra complex

According to legend, a king of Thebes called Laius was told by an oracle that if he had a son, that son would kill him. When his wife, Jocasta, gave birth to a baby boy, Laius tried to avoid his fate by leaving the child alone in the mountains to die.

But, with the help of some passing shepherds, the baby survived this attempted infanticide. Years later, the young Oedipus, as his adopted parents had called him, got into an argument with an old man driving a chariot and killed him in a fit of mythological roadrage.

Of course, the old man was Laius, Oedipus's real father. The prophecy was fulfilled at last. To make matters worse, Oedipus then proceeded to arrive in Thebes just in time to attract the attention of the newly widowed Jocasta. Not recognizing her, Oedipus married his own mother and became king of Thebes.

Sigmund Freud borrowed Oedipus's name at the beginning of the twentieth century to describe a supposed stage in a boy's development when he wishes to kill his father and have sex with his mother. This of course is very unfair to poor Oedipus, who wanted nothing of the sort. When he did eventually discover what he'd done, he was so mortified that he tore out his own eyes and spent the rest of his life wandering as a beggar, tormented by the Furies and by his own remorse.

OLYMPIC SPORT

One of the sports contested at the Olympic Games, as determined by the International Olympic Committee (IOC)

One of the unique features of ancient Greek society is the importance attached to athletics. All decent young men were expected to train regularly in the many gymnasia (from the Greek *gymnos*, meaning naked), which could be found in any ancient Greek city.

The most important of Greece's many athletic festivals was held every four years at the sanctuary of Zeus at Olympia. Athletes from all across the Greek world would come to these Olympic Games to try to win everlasting glory. Victors would become instant celebrities, immortalized in songs and poems by their admiring fans. Even warring nations would stop their fighting until the games were over.

When the Olympics were founded (traditionally said to be as long ago as 776 B.C.), there was only one event. Competitors would race in the nude over a simple straight track that was one *stadion* (about 650 feet or 200 m) in length (from which we get the modern word stadium).

The final ancient Olympics were held in A.D. 393 and the games were not revived again until 1896. Although the ancient Greeks gradually added extra events (including boxing, wrestling and chariot racing) to the original running competition, they would still have been baffled by the number and variety of modern Olympic sports. The idea of something like beach volleyball, played by *women,* who were allowed to wear *clothes,* would have seemed utterly ridiculous.

ORPHEUS

Anyone very skilled at music

The poet Orpheus was an ancient Greek mythological and religious figure, renowned as the greatest musician who ever lived. His songs, it was said, could charm the birds out of the sky and tame the wildest animals. Even the trees bowed down to listen. On the voyage of the Argonauts, Orpheus's music calmed the waves in front of the ship's prow, and when they passed the island of the Sirens, whose singing lured sailors to their deaths,

Orpheus saved the crew by singing a better song than even the immortal Sirens.

Orpheus had a beloved wife, Eurydice, who was killed by a snake bite while out walking. In desperation, the poet traveled down to the Underworld himself. He played his lyre so beautifully and so sadly that the guard dog Cerberus was lulled to sleep, and Queen Persephone agreed to let Eurydice return to life—with one condition: Eurydice would follow behind Orpheus up the long path to the light, but he was not to turn his head and look at her until they reached the surface.

As the pair were reaching the top, Orpheus, fearing a trick, turned around. He saw Eurydice climbing behind him but as his eyes fell on her she gasped and died a second time, never to return. Heartbroken, Orpheus abandoned the company of women, which so annoyed the local Thracian girls that, in a fit of madness, they set upon him and tore him to pieces. His severed head was thrown into a river and drifted out to sea, the stories say, still singing its tragic song.

TO BE OSTRACIZED

To be excluded or cast out from some group;
to be given the cold shoulder

The ancient Athenians, citizens of the world's first democracy, were intensely suspicious of anyone who looked as though they might be trying to seize too much power for themselves. In the turbulent political climate of ancient Greece, any successful politician could be a tyrant in waiting.

In order to curb their leaders' ambitions, the Athenians devised an unusual system called ostracism. Without giving any reason,

Athenians could vote to exile any politician from the city for ten years, after which they would be allowed to return. The votes were cast on shards of pottery known as *ostraka,* from which the modern word comes.

TO OPEN A PANDORA'S BOX

To unleash a stream of unforeseen problems;
to open a can of worms

According to the Greek poet Hesiod, Pandora was the world's first woman, created by the gods as a punishment for mankind. Pandora was blessed by the gods with all sorts of skills and graces, but beneath her extraordinary charms, they gave her a "shameless mind and a deceitful nature." At last, decked in Olympian finery, Pandora was given to the demigod Epimetheus as a wife.

Pandora brought with her a storage jar (later mistranslations made it a box), which the gods had filled with wars, plagues, famines and all the other evils in the world. When she arrived on Earth, Pandora, perhaps through curiosity or perhaps out of malice, lifted the lid and unleashed a torrent of troubles on mankind. Only one thing remained behind: Hope, which comforts people through all their misfortune.

In Hesiod's story, Pandora is an Eve-like figure who embodies the idea that women bring men nothing but trouble, and her name, which means all-gifts, refers to the many charming but deceptive qualities with which she is endowed. It's possible though that Pandora was originally a very ancient mother goddess, the "all-giver," who bestows both blessings and curses upon mankind.

P

PANPIPES

*A primitive instrument made of reeds or tubes
cut to different lengths*

In Greek mythology, Pan was a nature god associated with shepherds and woodland. When he wasn't asleep or hiding in the bushes spying on naked nymphs, Pan enjoyed playing on his pipe. This was a simple instrument—a set of different-sized reeds glued together—which he was said to have invented himself.

The story is that one day the excitable Pan was chasing a nymph called Syrinx with whom he'd fallen temporarily in love. In order to escape Pan's crude advances, Syrinx transformed herself into a reed, growing among the others along the banks of the Ladon River. Inspired by the sound of the wind sighing among the reed beds, Pan created the first panpipe, which he called a syrinx in honor of his lost love.

PANTOMIME

*A traditional English drama with a fairy-tale plot
and a strong emphasis on broad farcical comedy*

The ancient pantomime (from the Greek *pan,* or everything, and *mimesis*, or imitation) was a very popular form of dramatic entertain-

---

ANCIENT MUSICAL INSTRUMENTS

Ancient music was primarily focused on singing, but there were a few important varieties of musical instruments, as well as all sorts of percussion.

Brass—military brass bands were invented by the warlike Romans to accompany their constant military parades and shows. There were several kinds of brass instrument including the tuba, cornu (or "horn"), lituus and bucina.

The Lyre—a small, strummed harplike instrument made of strings stretched over a soundbox. It was associated with the god Apollo and with the performance of poetry.

The Pipes—the Greek auloi and Roman tibiae (the tibia, or shinbone, acquired its name because it looks like a pipe) were noisy instruments with a sound similar to the modern clarinet or bagpipe. They were associated with revelry and with the god Dionysus.

Water Organs—the first water organ, or hydraulis (from which we get the word "hydraulic"), was invented by an Alexandrian called Ctesibius during the third century B.C. These ancient marvels of engineering became very popular with the practically minded Romans.

---

ment in Imperial Rome. Accompanied by a chorus of singers and an orchestra who kept time with clappers attached to their feet, an actor or actress would use a succession of masks to dance out some melodramatic story, using gestures and hand movements to express the actions and emotions of its characters.

But the pantomime was certainly not family entertainment. The stories were usually mythological, but there was often a strong erotic element, which kept the patrons flooding in. Mime, which was very similar to pantomime, took this eroticism even further. At the festival of the Floralia, mime actresses would perform stripteases on stage, and the emperor Elagabalus (who was said to have murdered a room full of dinner guests by drowning them in rose petals) spiced up a traditional mime on the subject of adultery by insisting on realistic sex scenes.

PHILIPPIC

A fierce speech attacking something or someone

By the middle of the fourth century B.C., the ancient Greek city-states such as Thebes, Athens and Sparta were in decline. These great cities had been weakened by years of infighting and were now threatened by the emergence of the Macedonians to the north, led by King Philip II.

In Athens, the orator Demosthenes saw that unless the Greek cities could unite, they would be swept away by Macedonian power. In a series of speeches, he tried to rouse the Athenians to oppose Philip and his army. Demosthenes' speeches were called the Philippics, after the man they so relentlessly attacked.

Demosthenes' eloquence failed to stop Philip from conquering Greece, but his speeches lived on as classic examples of the art of rhetorical abuse. Hundreds of years later, when the Roman orator Cicero made speeches attacking Mark Antony, he named them Philippics in memory of Demosthenes' originals and the name has been applied to any impassioned attacking speech ever since.

PLATONIC RELATIONSHIP

A "pure" friendship that doesn't involve sexual feelings

The philosophy of Plato is preserved in his *Dialogues,* written in Athens during the fourth century B.C. One of the most famous is

The Symposium, which tells the story of an extraordinary dinner party attended by some of the leading figures of Classical Athens. Over the course of the evening, the increasingly drunken guests have a profound discussion about the true nature of love.

The most distinguished guest was the philosopher Socrates who, for all his notable qualities, was not one of nature's handsomest specimens. He was, records Plato, a coarse-looking individual who went around the city barefoot and avoided baths.

Despite these eccentricities of personal hygiene, it isn't long before he is fending off the advances of no less a person than Alcibiades, a society charmer who was famous as one of the best-looking young men in the city. Alcibiades had perceived the extraordinary wisdom that lurked behind Socrates' brutish exterior and confessed that he was totally smitten.

But this wasn't Alcibiades' lucky night. Socrates, Plato reports, has discovered the higher truth of love, which rises above mere physical lust to become a pure love based on true inner and spiritual beauty. This Platonic love was a deep and philosophical passion, but it's the fact that there was no sex that is remembered in the term's usage today.

TO BE IN A PRIAPIC CONDITION

To be in a state of sexual excitement

Priapus was a primitive fertility god, first worshipped in the Lampsacus region of northwestern Turkey. He was the protector of gardens, vineyards and orchards and was honored for his ability to ward off the evil eye. Priapus was traditionally said to be the son of Aphrodite and Dionysus, but according to one mythological tradition, he was a son of Aphrodite and Zeus. Jealous of her husband's affairs, Zeus's wife, Hera, cursed the infant with grotesquely oversized genitals and a permanent erection, attributes depicted in representations of him in ancient art. Among the Romans, statues of Priapus, which were thought to encourage fertility, were popular garden ornaments—a sort of X-rated equivalent to today's garden gnomes.

In modern medicine, priapism is a condition in which a man maintains an unwanted erection for several hours or even days. It can be very painful and in extreme cases leads to amputation of the affected part.

PROMETHEAN CUNNING

*Superhuman cunning, especially when deployed
in the service of science or craft*

Prometheus, whose name means forward thinker, was an important Greek demigod, famous for his intelligence and for being a trickster, but also for being one of the great benefactors of mankind. Some versions of his story even credit him with having created the first humans, using clay and animal parts.

Prometheus's rebellious streak ensured that his relationship with his cousin Zeus was always rather stormy. On one occasion, Prometheus divided a sacrificed ox into two piles. In one pile were all the bones and entrails, but they were covered in a layer of tasty meat. In the other were all the finest cuts, concealed under the cow's stomach. Zeus was tricked into choosing the attractive but worthless part of the sacrifice for the immortal gods, while mortals were left with the good part.

The final straw came when Prometheus stole sacred fire from Olympus for his mortal protégés to cook their steaks on, which was in direct violation of Zeus's divine edict. Enraged by this latest act of defiance, Zeus had Prometheus chained to a rock in the Caucasus Mountains, where a colossal vulture would come and tear out his divine innards with its beak. Every night, his immortal organs would painfully grow back, only to be mutilated again the following morning.

TO BE PROTEAN

To have an amazing ability to change or adapt

In Greek mythology, Proteus was one of several minor deities associated with the sea. It is believed he lived on the island of Pharos, near the mouth of the Nile, where he was responsible for tending herds of sea creatures for Poseidon.

Proteus was blessed with the ability to see the future, but those who came to seek his advice found the god remarkably hard to pin down. At the mere sight of a needy mortal, Proteus would deploy his other remarkable talent: the ability to transform himself into any form he could imagine.

PYGMALION

A man who "creates" a woman by teaching her
to adopt some persona

In Greek mythology, Pygmalion was a king of Cyprus who, according to Ovid's *Metamorphoses,* carved an ivory statue of a woman that was so beautiful that he fell in love with it. Full of passion, the king neglected all living girls, gazing for hours at his statue's chilly perfection. The love-struck sculptor was in danger of entirely wasting away until the goddess Aphrodite generously transformed the statue into a real woman, whom he made his queen.

In modern usage, Pygmalion is generally a reference to the play by George Bernard Shaw, who produced an imaginative reinterpretation of the Greek myth. His story of a linguistics professor who "creates" a respectable lady out of a loudmouthed Englishwoman became a worldwide hit when it was filmed as *My Fair Lady*.

PYRRHIC VICTORY

A victory that comes at too great a cost

Pyrrhus (319–272 B.C.), king of Epirus in northwest Greece, was one of the greatest generals of the ancient world, and he was one of the few men to have successfully defeated a Roman army in battle. He was said to be a direct descendant of Achilles. With a small army of mercenaries, including war elephants, Pyrrhus destroyed superior Roman forces at two battles in southern Italy and advanced toward Rome.

But Pyrrhus's victories had been hard fought and he had no way of replacing the quality troops he had lost in the bloody fighting. Although he came within a few miles of Rome, his army was too weakened to storm the city walls. Meanwhile, the beaten Romans were quietly drawing on their endless reserves of manpower, and before long they were able to face Pyrrhus's depleted army in battle again, finally driving him out of Italy for good.

The phrase "Pyrrhic Victory" comes from a story that is told of Pyrrhus after the battle of Asculum in 279 B.C. To someone congratulating him on his victory over the Roman legions, Pyrrhus replied: "One more victory like that and I'll be ruined!"

PYTHON

A genus of large, nonvenomous, tropical snake

In Greek mythology, Python was the name of a giant snake or dragon that lived near Delphi and had the power to see the future. It was said to have been the guardian of the monstrous giant Typhon. When the god Apollo wanted to set up his own oracle at Delphi, the first thing he did was kill the Python with arrows to eliminate a rival in the prophetic arts. In memory of this killing, Apollo at Delphi was known as Pythian Apollo, and the oracular priestesses who interpreted the god's instructions for men were often referred to as the pythonesses.

R

RED-LETTER DAY

A special occasion or anniversary

Instead of dividing their lives into weeks and weekends, the ancient Romans littered their calendar with a huge number of religious festivals. On these sacred days, no official business was allowed to take place and the city of Rome would grind to a halt as the people gathered at the temples to drink wine and sacrifice animals to the gods.

Sometimes there were grand parades, such as the Lupercalia in February when aristocratic youths would run naked through the crowd, striking women with leather thongs. Sometimes there were important rituals, for example, during the Lemuria, when Romans threw beans over their shoulders to appease the hungry dead.

By the middle of the Imperial period of Rome's history, there were so many festivals that they took up nearly half the year and made it almost impossible to get anything done. The emperor Marcus Aurelius was forced to pass a law limiting the number of festival days to a still remarkable 135.

But amid this endless celebration, some really important festivals still stood out from the crowd, most likely because they were sometimes marked in Roman calendars with special red ink. This practice was transferred, after the end of paganism, to the important festivals of the early Christian calendar—the first red-letter days.

TO REST ON YOUR LAURELS

To be content with the success you have already achieved and not strive for more

In Greek mythology, Daphne was a nymph who was pursued by the god Apollo and, to escape his advances, she transformed herself into a laurel tree (or *daphnê* in Greek). In memory of the nymph, the ancient Greeks held the laurel to be sacred to Apollo, and laurel wreaths were presented to winning athletes at Apollo's Pythian games.

In wider Greek culture, laurel leaves became common symbols of victory. Meanwhile in Rome, laurels were awarded to generals who defeated enemies in battle. Even today the plant's association with success lives on in words, such as baccalaureate and Poet Laureate.

RHETORICAL QUESTION

*A question asked for dramatic effect,
with no expectation of an answer*

The art of rhetoric, or public speaking, was considered one of the most important skills an educated Greek or Roman could acquire. In democratic Athens and republican Rome, careers could be made or broken on the basis of one good speech, and men like Demosthenes or Cicero used their words to a devastating effect.

The Greeks, who never missed an opportunity to write a treatise on something, quickly developed rhetoric into a high science. Aristotle wrote an entire *Ars Rhetorica,* and schools of rhetoric sprang up all over the ancient world, where pupils would be coached in stylistic tricks or taught to enunciate with pebbles in their mouths. All aspects of a speech were subject to intense scrutiny: One Roman politician, Gaius Gracchus, had a slave standing by with a flute whenever he spoke, in case he needed to moderate his pitch.

As democracy and republic gave way to empire, the practical use of rhetoric declined, but it remained popular. Constant flattery toward the emperors made panegyrics (speeches in praise of things) a popular genre. By the late empire, the art that had evolved in the bracing and serious atmosphere of ancient democracy was being used to refine speeches, such as Eulogy for a Gnat, or In Praise of Hair. What Demosthenes would have thought of that, we can only begin to imagine.

RICH AS CROESUS

Extremely wealthy

Croesus was a king of Lydia in central Turkey who ruled *c.* 560 to 546 B.C. The kingdom, which already had rich natural gold deposits, had its treasuries boosted by tribute from the Greek cities to the west, and Croesus became famous for his wealth and power.

The Greeks, always fond of moralizing about how pride comes before a fall, loved to tell the unlikely but popular story of Croesus's meeting with the Athenian legislator Solon. According to the story, the Athenian punctured Croesus's glow of wealthy self-satisfaction with the famous line: "Call no man happy until he is dead." As Solon knew, there's nothing the gods like better than to give a man a glimpse of happiness and then plunge him into ruin. So it's foolish to count anyone lucky until you know that their good fortune wasn't just a flash in the pan.

Croesus, secure in his power, laughed off the warning. However, many years later he was defeated in battle and captured by a Persian army. He is said to have alarmed onlookers by crying "Solon! Solon!"as he was ceremonially burned alive amid the devastated ruins of his capital.

ROSTRUM

A speaker's platform or pulpit

Even while Roman armies were advancing throughout the Mediterranean world, the politics of the Republic remained obstinately focused on the city of Rome. The lives and affairs of thousands of people in the many far-flung provinces were bent to the whims of the squabbling senatorial elite of one central Italian city.

R

At the heart of this city's politics was the speaker's platform, called the *rostra*, named after the prows (in Latin, a *rostrum* is a beak or prow) of defeated Carthaginian warships that were displayed as trophies nearby. The aristocratic senators would use this platform to address their policies and arguments to the crowd face to face. This was politics at its most direct and confrontational, where the rulers and the ruled could fight (and physical violence was not unheard of) over the future of the city—a far cry from the tame speeches we get from rostrums today.

S

TO SAIL BETWEEN SCYLLA AND CHARYBDIS

*To be trapped between two bad alternatives;
between a rock and a hard place*

During his ten-year wanderings on the way home from Troy, the hero Odysseus was forced to sail through a narrow passage of water that was home to a particularly notorious pair of mythical monsters: Scylla and Charybdis.

Charybdis was a daughter of Gaia and Poseidon who was, because of her excessive greed, cursed by Zeus to stand forever at the bottom of the sea, sucking vast quantities of water into her belly and then vomiting it up again. Vessels that passed too close would be dragged down into her cavernous mouth, never to be seen again.

To avoid risking his entire ship in Charybdis's whirlpool, Odysseus steered toward the cliffs on the opposite side of the strait. Unfortunately for him, these cliffs were the home of Scylla, a nymph who, due to another divine curse, had six terrifying dogs growing out of her groin. These ravenous hounds stretched over the side of Odysseus's ship, snatched up six of his best sailors in their jaws and carried them back to the rocks, where their grim mistress could devour them at her leisure.

SAPPHIC PRACTICES

Female homosexuality

Sappho was a Greek lyric poet who was born on the island of Lesbos toward the end of the seventh century B.C. This makes her one of Greek literature's earliest figures, as well as one of its most extraordinary.

Sadly only fragments of Sappho's poetry have survived the passage of time, and historians can only build a vague and incomplete picture of Sappho's life. Many of the fragments come from passionate love poems, which appear to be written by Sappho to other girls.

Although male homosexuality was generally accepted in ancient Greek society, at least within certain boundaries, female sexuality of any sort was hardly believed to exist at all; women didn't do sex—they had it done to them. Presumably, thought classical commentators, Sappho's love was very much of the intellectual, spiritual kind.

Two and a half thousand years later, it's impossible to know what kind of love really went on between Sappho and her circle. But that didn't stop the Victorians from stealing her name when they needed a nice genteel euphemism for "unspeakable goings-on" between women. Even the name of Sappho's island—Lesbos—was used, giving us the modern word lesbian.

SATURNALIAN REVELS

A wild party, especially one in which normal rules are overturned

The Saturnalia was a festival in honor of the Roman god Saturn, which took place every year at the end of December. Even for a Roman festival the Saturnalia was known for being particularly riotous and debauched. Most bizarre of all, for an extremely class-ridden society like that of ancient Rome, the normal rules of hierarchy were reversed. Slaves could give orders to senators and servants bossed their masters around—in theory at least, if not in practice. For those few days, the whole of Roman society was turned on its head.

SATURNINE

Gloomy, glowering or dull

The word saturnine originally referred to those born under the sign of Saturn, who were thought to be predisposed toward melancholic qualities. The planet Saturn is named after the Roman god of the same name, who was one of the oldest deities of the Roman Pantheon. The Romans identified Saturn with the Greek god Cronus, but Saturn probably existed in Roman mythology long before it became tangled up with Greek. He was often depicted with a scythe, was sometimes regarded as a god of the Underworld and may be part of the inspiration for the familiar modern caricature figure of Death.

A SHIRT OF NESSUS

A source of torment that can't be escaped; a fatal gift

In Greek mythology, Nessus was a centaur who tried to rape Deianeira, the second wife of Heracles. Since Heracles was the greatest hero ancient Greece had ever seen, this was always bound to backfire, and, before long, Heracles had duly appeared and shot Nessus dead with one of his poisoned arrows.

But Nessus had a final cruel trick up his sleeve. With his dying breath, he told Deianeira that a mixture of his blood and the semen he had expelled during the rape attempt would, if smeared on one of Heracles' garments, cause the hero to love her forever. Eager to make sure of her man, Deianeira faithfully followed the centaur's instructions.

Of course, as Nessus had known, his blood was still full of the hydra venom that Heracles used on his arrows and when Heracles put the shirt on, the poison burned agonizingly into his skin. Worse still, the shirt clung to his body, so that as he tried to remove it he tore off great strips of flesh. At last, to end his hideous suffering, Greece's greatest hero rushed into a fire and burned himself alive.

You've been using that irritating laundry detergent again ...

SIREN VOICES

Seductive tempters who lead you to disaster

The Sirens were creatures of Greek mythology who had the faces and necks of beautiful girls and the bodies of monstrous birds. Sitting on the shore of their island, the Sirens used to make music so beautiful that sailors passing by would steer their ships straight onto the jagged rocks just to be close to the source of their wonderful song. Still singing, the Sirens would feast on the bodies of the drowning men.

According to legend, Odysseus heard the song of the Sirens on his long journey home from Troy. Luckily for him, the witch Circe had forewarned him about the   powers. Following her instructions, the cunning hero ordered his men to block their own ears with beeswax and to tie him firmly to the ship's mast before they passed the island.

As soon as Odysseus heard the famous song, he was seized with the desire to leap overboard and swim to the makers of this divine music. But he couldn't break the ropes that bound him and, despite all his threats and pleading, his men refused to let him go until they had sailed safely by. Meanwhile, the infuriated Sirens promptly leaped into the sea and drowned themselves, like offended prima donnas.

SISYPHEAN TASK

A seemingly pointless, impossible or never-ending task

Sisyphus was a mythological king of Ephyra in Greece, who was famous for his cunning, a quality that he usually used to prolong his own life. On one occasion he kidnapped the spirit of Death by tricking him into testing a set of magical chains. Even when Sisyphus was finally dragged down to the Underworld it wasn't long before he wheedled his way up again.

Eventually Zeus caught up with the crafty king and sent him to Tartarus, the lowest region of the Underworld and the ancient Greek equivalent of hell, where his punishment was to spend eternity rolling a round boulder up a mountain. Every so often Sisyphus would manage to heave the great stone to the top, where it would topple over and roll down the other side, all the way back to the bottom.

In the Classical era, Sisyphus served as a warning to mortals of the dangers of trying to outwit the immortal gods. But in the twentieth century, Sisyphus was reinvented as an absurdist hero. The French writer Albert Camus called him the "proletarian of the gods" and admired the unfortunate king for his lucidity and scorn.

SOCRATIC METHOD

A method of debate in which seemingly innocent questions are asked to try to expose the weaknesses in someone else's argument

Socrates was an Athenian philosopher who lived from 469 to 399 B.C. He became perhaps the most famous philosopher in the classical world and has inspired thinkers ever since.

Everything we know about Socrates comes from ancient accounts of his life rather than his own writings. A main source is Plato's Dialogues which are, supposedly, records of real conversations that Socrates had with other contemporary philosophers. A picture emerges of a very bright inquiring mind, who was a nightmare to argue against. Any thinker who passed through Athens would soon bump into Socrates, perhaps at a drunken dinner party or out and about in the city with his friends.

Before long, Socrates would draw the visitor into discussion, humbly asking him to expound his ideas on beauty or virtue or some other elevated topic. Then, by asking him to clarify this or expand on that, Socrates would tease out the contradictions in his argument, never saying them outright but subtly bending the conversation so that his opponent would stumble upon them himself.

Although this was a great way to advance toward philosophical truth, it was also pretty annoying. Following the Athenian defeat in the Peloponnesian War, the grumpy populace took out some of their collective angst on the unfortunate philosopher, condemning him to death by poison on charges of atheism and corrupting young men.

SOPHISTRY

Spurious but clever-seeming argument or conversation

In ancient Greece, the sophists were traveling teachers who would instruct young men in philosophy, rhetoric and mathematics for a fee. As the city of Athens rose to power and prominence in the fifth century B.C., so sophists from across Greece arrived in the city in large numbers, offering their services to those who could afford it.

In Athenian democracy, the art of rhetoric, or public speaking, was thought to be particularly important, and it received special attention from sophistic teachers. Exercises such as the famous *dissoi logoi*, in which pupils were encouraged to argue both sides of the same case, helped train young men for the cut and thrust of Athenian political life.

But this emphasis on style over substance provoked a serious backlash. The comedian Aristophanes wrote a whole play, *The Clouds,* about sophists who teach invincible but hollow arguments in their "thinkery," enabling a young man to persuade a jury into anything he wants and get away with all sorts of disgraceful behavior. Plato, too, wrote powerfully against the sophists' alleged moral flexibility.

These Athenian writings mean that these days "sophistry" is associated with trickiness and pointless complication, a reputation that isn't entirely deserved. The thinking of the sophists is better reflected by another word that comes from the same root: sophistication.

TO SOW DRAGON'S TEETH

To plant the seeds of future conflict

The idea of sowing dragon's teeth comes from the story of Cadmus, the legendary founder of the city of Thebes.

In order to establish his new city, Cadmus fought and killed a local dragon, sacred to Ares, who was living by a nearby spring. Acting on the advice of the goddess Athena, the hero cut out the dead dragon's teeth and planted them in the soil.

Darn! All that trouble and it had dentures.

Immediately, these grisly seeds began to bear fruit. To Cadmus's horror, wherever a tooth had been planted, a ferocious-looking warrior started sprouting out of the ground. Each was fully armed with shield and spear. Fearing another battle, Cadmus picked up a rock and threw it into the throng.

This strategy worked surprisingly well. Each of the tooth-men—who seem to be better at fighting than at thinking—assumed that one of the others was pelting him with stones. Before long, the newly grown men were busily trying their best to put each other back in the ground, while Cadmus looked on happily from the sidelines. Eventually, when the surviving tooth-men were too exhausted to fight any longer, they joined with Cadmus to populate his new nation.

I'M SPARTACUS

*An attempt to take blame for something
one didn't do; a gesture of defiance*

In the year 73 B.C., in the last years of the Roman Republic, a Thracian gladiator called Spartacus set off the most dangerous revolt in Rome's history. With a group of fellow gladiators, he broke out of confinement and made for Mount Vesuvius, gathering men as he went. A strong force of two legions sent to crush the uprising was comprehensively beaten, and so was a second force soon after. In the end it took an army of six full legions to put an end to the rebellion.

The famous line "I'm Spartacus" is taken from the end of the 1960 film *Spartacus,* starring Kirk Douglas. The gladiator and his remaining men are captured by the Romans, who offer to spare them if they will point out which of them is Spartacus. As

Spartacus moves to reveal himself, he finds that all his men are also claiming his name, refusing to let him die alone.

It's a great movie moment, but the historical Romans certainly weren't interested in sparing anyone after the Spartacus revolt. Roman society, based on the labor of vast numbers of slaves, had been badly shaken by the daring of the thousands who had fought for freedom so, as a warning to others, the survivors were crucified to a man.

SPARTAN CONDITIONS

Harsh, uncomfortable surroundings

The Spartans of Laconia in southern Greece took warfare very seriously. From the very first moment, a Spartan man's life was a boot camp designed to turn him into the perfect fighting machine. Parents of Spartan babies would bathe their newborns in wine to toughen them up, and weaklings would be left out as food for the wolves up on Mount Taygetus.

At the age of seven, boys were put into state-run barracks to begin a training regime that included wilderness survival, organized fights and lots of whipping. There was never enough food, so the cadets had to steal to survive, although the punishments for getting caught were severe. According to the Greek historian Plutarch, one boy hid a stolen fox cub under his shirt and didn't make a sound while the angry animal bit him to death.

Even as adults, Spartans continued to live most of their lives in army messes, telling war stories and eating a notoriously unpleasant kind of porridge. It was a grim existence, but it did have the desired effect: Spartan soldiers were unstoppable in a fight. Their extraordinary courage during the Persian Wars at battles such as Plataea in 479 B.C. and Thermopylae in 480 B.C. (where three hundred Spartans, along with some allied contingents, held off an enormous Persian army) became the stuff of legend.

A SPHINXLIKE SMILE

A mysterious, inscrutable or secretive smile

In Greek mythology, the Sphinx was a monster with the head of a woman but the body of a lion and the wings of a bird of prey, whose lair lay by a road near the city of Thebes. Her favorite trick was to ask travelers a riddle where the penalty for answering wrong was to be eaten alive.

The first and only person ever to get the Sphinx's riddle right was Oedipus, on his way to Thebes after accidentally killing his father. The Sphinx asked what creature has sometimes three legs, sometimes two legs and sometimes four legs and is strongest when its legs are fewest. The answer, as Oedipus saw, is a human—the only animal that crawls as a baby, walks upright as an adult and, when it gets old, moves with the aid of a stick. When the Sphinx found that her riddle had been answered, she was so disgusted that she hurled herself off a rock and died.

TO SPRING FROM ONE'S HEAD FULLY FORMED

To appear suddenly from nowhere without any process of development—especially of ideas

In Greek mythology, the politics of heaven were often as unstable as any down on Earth. The first chief god, Uranus, was toppled by his son, Cronus. Cronus was toppled by Zeus. So it was no surprise to anyone when it was foretold that if Zeus had a son by his first wife Metis, the daughter of the Titans Oceanus and Tethys, that son would be his father's ruin. This was particularly worrying since Metis was already pregnant with Zeus's child so, to prevent disaster, Zeus chose the traditional chief-god approach and swallowed Metis alive, along with her unborn baby. After this, all was quiet until one day Zeus found himself with a splitting headache that wouldn't go away. Finally, to relieve the pain, he asked Hephaestus to split open the offending part of his skull with an axe.

The unorthodox treatment turned out be remarkably effective. As soon as Zeus's skull was cut, the source of the problem became clear. From inside Zeus's head leaped a mighty goddess in shining armor, crying a loud war cry that shook the heavens.

This goddess was the daughter of Zeus, whom her mother had borne inside her father's belly. She became known as Athena, goddess of war and patroness of the arts and of the city of Athens, which bears her name.

A STENTORIAN ROAR

A very loud shout

Stentor was a Thracian herald who was described briefly in Homer's *Iliad* as being able to shout as loudly as fifty men. This would have proved a useful talent in the fighting around Troy, but as often happens in Greek mythology, Stentor let himself get carried away by his success and found himself in a shouting match with the god Hermes, herald of the Olympians. Unsurprisingly, Stentor lost and was put to death for even thinking about comparing himself to one of the immortals.

STOIC ENDURANCE

The art of calmly accepting whatever misfortune life throws at you

Stoicism was a Greek philosophical school of thought, which was founded by Zeno of Citium (in Cyprus) around 300 B.C. and achieved great popularity among the Romans in the centuries that followed. Among other things, Stoic philosophy taught that the world was supremely good. Things that looked bad from an individual perspective—poverty, bereavement, disease—would be seen as good if the sufferer could just see the bigger picture.

This philosophy meant that Stoics were very good at enduring pain and misfortune. Even death was turned into a sort of Stoic art form, where expiring gracefully became a matter of philosophical pride. Accounts of great Stoic deaths were passed down as an inspiration to future generations.

One of the most famous deaths was the forced suicide of Seneca the Younger. Condemned to die by Nero, the philosopher set his worldly affairs in order, gave his wife a parting kiss and, with his friends around him, cut the arteries of both wrists. Finding himself still alive some minutes later, Seneca cut the arteries of his legs, too, but his body still obstinately refused to die. A dose of poison was similarly ineffective, and things were looking bleak until he managed finally to suffocate himself in a steaming hot bath. Of course, all through this hideous ordeal, the philosopher was calmly regaling his assembled disciples with philosophical maxims and friendly advice.

TO STRIKE LIKE A THUNDERBOLT

*To occur suddenly and forcefully, especially
of emotions, ideas, and realizations*

In the ancient world, if someone was struck by a thunderbolt it was a sure sign that he or she had displeased Zeus, the king of the gods. Thunderbolts were Zeus's particular weapon, an association dating back to the earliest period of Greek religion when Zeus was regarded primarily as a sky-god rather than the all-encompassing father figure he later became.

Zeus first gained control of the thunderbolt when he needed a weapon to overthrow his divine father, Cronus. Foolishly, Cronus had made an enemy of the Cyclopes, the monstrous creatures famous for their skill at metalwork. Released by Zeus from confinement in the pit of Tartarus, the Cyclopes forged the thunderbolt for him in the fires of Mount Etna, and Zeus was able to use it to strike his father down.

Since his first experiment with thunderbolt striking had allowed him to take over Olympus, Zeus saw no reason not to keep up the good work. So over the years, quite a few people found themselves struck by his bolts from the blue. To ancient Greeks, for whom getting struck by a thunderbolt was a genuine religious concern, our modern idiom probably would seem dangerously lighthearted.

TO BE STRUCK BY CUPID'S ARROW

To fall in love

In Roman religion, Cupid was the personification of amorous obsession. His name in Latin simply means desire.

The Romans—at least the romantic ones—imagined him as a

child armed with a bow and arrows, which he would shoot into the hearts of his victims. Those who were pierced by the arrows would fall immediately and helplessly in love. Like a child, Cupid could be kind and playful, but as a god, he was also prone to casual acts of cruelty.

One of his most famous victims was the Carthaginian queen Dido, who, according to Virgil's *Aeneid,* was tricked into cradling the disguised Cupid in her arms. This close encounter with the love god caused the queen to develop an uncontrollable passion for the Trojan hero Aeneas. He, in typical masculine style, was happy to take advantage for a time, but eventually took off to fulfill his destiny. The heartbroken Dido, driven mad by Cupid, hurled herself onto a burning funeral pyre.

In the modern world, the image of a heart pierced by Cupid's arrow has become a popular symbol of love. Cupid can be seen, with his bow, carved in bronze in the middle of London's Piccadilly Circus.

STYGIAN GLOOM

Menacing, oppressive darkness

The word Stygian means "relating to the River Styx," probably the most famous of the five rivers that were believed by the ancient Greeks to run through the Underworld and separate the land of the dead from the land of the living. The River Styx derives its name from the Greek word for hatred, and it became a powerful symbol of the grim horrors of the ancient afterlife. The poet Dante, writing during the Renaissance, imagined the Styx as a murky black swamp where the angry and the sullen are confined as perpetual punishment.

The River Styx was sacred even among the Olympian gods. When a god wanted to swear the most sacred possible oath, he or she would swear on the River Styx. Any god who broke such an oath would be unable to eat, drink or even breathe for an entire year and was banished from the company of the gods for a another nine.

SWORD OF DAMOCLES

A disaster waiting to happen; a threat that hangs
over you and causes anxiety

This expression comes from a story about the Sicilian tyrant Dionysius II that was told by the great Roman orator Cicero. Dionysius, wrote Cicero, was once told by a flattering courtier called Damocles that, with all the wealth and luxury surrounding him, he must be the luckiest ruler in the world. To teach Damocles a lesson, Dionysius challenged the courtier to take his place on the throne for one evening to see how much he enjoyed the pleasures of kingship.

Sitting on his golden couch, being fed the finest food and wine by the handsomest servants, Damocles initially thought that being a tyrant was a pretty decent sort of lifestyle. However, glancing upwards, he noticed to his horror that there was a sword hanging directly above his head, pointing downward and suspended from the ceiling by a single hair.

Unsurprisingly, Damocles found that the constant possibility of being skewered like a kebab did put him off from his food. Dionysius's point, and Cicero's, was that with power and luxury comes constant danger, and happiness can only be achieved with an untroubled mind. In modern usage, "sword of Damocles" tends simply to indicate a disaster that constantly threatens but never comes.

T

TO BE TANTALIZING

*To be extremely tempting or appealing,
but always forbidden or just out of reach*

During his lifetime, the legendary King Tantalus was one of the gods' most favored mortals, and the Olympians could often be found feasting with him in his palace. However, he clearly allowed all this admiration to go to his head, because he soon started indulging in some very risky misbehavior.

Some say Tantalus spread confidential gossip that he'd heard at divine dinner parties. Others claim that he stole Zeus' dog. Most seriously, he is alleged to have boiled his own son, Pelops, in a stew and served him to his immortal guests. Either way, the king was condemned by the gods to spend eternity in Tartarus, the Greek equivalent of our hell.

In Tartarus, Tantalus was tormented with terrible hunger and thirst. Worse still, the famished king was forced to stand forever in a pool of water, beneath a tree bearing delicious fruit. Whenever Tantalus bent down to wet his parched mouth, the water would disappear in front of him, and whenever he lifted his arm to take a fruit, the branches would rise out of his reach.

TO BE A TITAN

To be a giant in your field; to be superhumanly powerful or strong

According to the Greek poet Hesiod, the first gods to appear from Chaos were Uranus (Sky) and Gaia (Earth). These two had six sons and six daughters who were known as the Titans. The youngest was Cronus who castrated his father with a sickle and threw his severed genitals into the sea. Emasculated in the most literal possible way, Uranus stepped aside and allowed his twelve children to rule the roost.

But the dominance of the Titans didn't last long. Cronus had several children, and the youngest, Zeus, rebelled against his father. After a ten-year war called the Titanomachy, he toppled Cronus as supreme god. Zeus and his siblings became known as the Olympian gods, after Mount Olympus where they made their home.

The Titans were much more elemental and less human by nature than the Olympian gods: Oceanus, for example, personified the world's oceans, while Hyperion was also the sun. So, titanic became a word to describe things that were vast, impressive and strong, most notoriously the "unsinkable" ship that struck an iceberg and sank in 1912. If only the shipbuilders had thought harder about the fate of the original Titans, they might have realized the truth of the old saying: Pride comes before a fall.

TRAGEDY

An extremely sad occurrence

Tragedy was an ancient dramatic genre that became one of Greece's most important forms of artistic expression. In modern usage, we've come to apply the word tragedy to all sorts of relatively minor mishaps. This would have seemed very odd to the ancient Greeks,

THE 12 TITANS

Coeus—grandfather of Apollo and Artemis

Crius—grandfather of Hecate, the goddess of witchcraft and crossroads

Cronus—youngest son of Uranus and Gaia; became chief of the gods after castrating his father with a flint sickle

Hyperion—father of the sun-god Helios; the moon-goddess Selene; and Eos, the spirit of the dawn

Iapetus—father of the giant Atlas, as well as the famous trickster Prometheus and his brother Epimetheus

Mnemosyne—personification of memory and mother of the Muses

Oceanus—eldest of the Titans; personification of the great river that the Greeks believed circled the earth

Phoebe—associated with the moon; wife of Coeus and grandmother of Apollo and Artemis

Rhea—wife of Cronus and mother to Hera, Hades, Poseidon and Zeus, among others

Theia– wife of Hyperion

Themis—goddess of law and mother of the fates; one of the early wives of Zeus, who was also her nephew

Tethys—wife of Oceanus and personification of the fertility of the sea; said to have had more than three thousand children

whose tragedies generally had a dash of divine madness, a sprinkling of incest, a high body count and a lot of wailing.

The genre was invented around the sixth century B.C., and it quickly achieved huge popularity. The word, which comes from *tragos,* meaning goat, and *aeidô,* meaning to sing, dates back to times when tragedies were just songs, perhaps performed in competition, with a goat as the prize.

By the end of the fifth century B.C., tragedy had become a very big deal. The Athenian drama festival, the Dionysia, attracted huge crowds, and tragedies by the three greatest writers, Aeschylus, Sophocles and Euripides, are still being performed today.

A TRITON AMONG MINNOWS

*Someone who is superior to his peers;
a big fish in a small pond*

In Greek mythology, Triton was one of several minor deities associated with the sea. His role in legend is fairly small. He was said to have helped the Argonauts to cross Lake Tritonis in Libya and to have lost a fight with Dionysus, and he sometimes features as the father of Pallas who was killed by Athena, but generally Triton, like the other gods of the deep, seems to have preferred to keep himself to himself.

In later legend, Triton began to be thought of as one of many Tritons, fishtailed mermen in the retinue of Poseidon, often depicted holding conch shells and tridents. This definitely represented something of a demotion, but at least Tritons were still better than the minnows with which they have been proverbially compared. The last twist in Triton's fortunes came in the nineteenth century when astronomers used his name for one of the moons of Neptune.

TRIUMPH

A notable success

In ancient Rome, a triumph was a very prestigious victory parade that could be held by only the most successful generals. Dressed in

DEITIES OF THE SEA

As a people who depended on the sea for trade and livelihood, the Greeks honored a huge number of sea gods. Some of the most important are:

Glaucus—gained immortality from a magic herb; became a fish-tailed sea god and lover of Scylla

Glaucus, son of Sisyphus—gained immortality by drinking at a sacred fountain and threw himself in the sea to prove it; for sailors to see him was a sign of impending death

The Harpies—Aello, Ocypete and Celaeno; monstrous personifications of the stormy sea

The Nereids—sea nymphs, daughters of Nereus

Nereus—old man of the sea, benevolent protector of sailors

Oceanus—Titan and personification of the river Ocean

The Oceanids—the 3,000 daughters of Oceanus and Tethys

Phorcys—an ancient sea god; father of Echidna, the Gorgons and the Graiae

Poseidon (Neptune)—all-powerful god of the seas and of earthquakes, brother of Zeus

Proteus—a god of the sea, charged with looking after Poseidon's herds of seals and other sea creatures; famous for changing his form at will

Tethys—a Titan of the sea, wife of Oceanus and mother of the rivers

Thetis—a Nereid, wife of Peleus and mother of Achilles

Triton—god of Lake Tritonis, archetype of the Tritons or mermen

the ancient regalia of the Etruscan kings, the triumphant general would enter the city on a four-horse chariot, decked with a victory laurel, and fitted with a ceremonial wooden phallus on its underside. Following behind came the victorious legionaries, along with their miserable captives who were paraded as trophies in front of the Roman people.

To prevent these regal trappings from going to anyone's head, a tradition arose that the general would have a slave standing behind him on his chariot, who would repeat, over and over, "remember you are only a man." And to bring down his pride even further, the exuberant troops were allowed, perhaps even encouraged, to sing rude songs about their general as they marched by. At Julius Caesar's triumphs his legionaries sang, among other things, that he'd lost his virginity to the king of Bithynia, and that he'd spent most of his Gallic campaign chasing prostitutes.

> Here we bring our bald whoremonger;
> Romans lock your wives away!
> All the bags of gold you lent him
> Went his Gallic tarts to pay.
> —Fragment from a triumphal song about Julius Caesar,
> according to Suetonius, trans. Robert Graves

Despite the embarrassing songs, a triumph was a huge honor that was awarded for only the greatest victories. Most generals had to manage with a lesser ceremony called an *ovatio* (from which we get "standing ovation").

TROJAN HORSE

A trick used to bypass someone's defenses by stealth

By the tenth year of the Greeks' legendary siege of Troy, things seemed to have reached a stalemate. Many of the greatest heroes on each side were dead. Achilles had killed Hector. Paris had killed Achilles. Philoctetes had killed Paris. But Troy's great walls remained as solid as they had always been.

It was at this point, according to Virgil's *Aeneid,* that the Trojans woke up one morning to find that the besieging army had disappeared. Left behind on the beach where their camp had been was a huge wooden horse, which, after some deliberation, the Trojans wheeled into the city thinking that it was an offering to the gods.

But hiding inside the horse was a band of Greek troops, led by the fearsome Odysseus, who, when night fell, climbed down from its wooden belly and opened the gates of Troy. Meanwhile, the rest of the Greek army, which had been hiding out at sea, returned to take advantage of the breach in Troy's defenses. The Trojans, caught by surprise after a night of celebration and feasting, were slaughtered; their city was burned to the ground; and their women were taken as slaves by the conquering Greeks.

Ancient interpreters, doubting the legend, often explained the Trojan horse as a type of siege engine or battering ram. In modern usage, Trojan Horse is also used as a name for a computer virus that infects a system by pretending to be useful software.

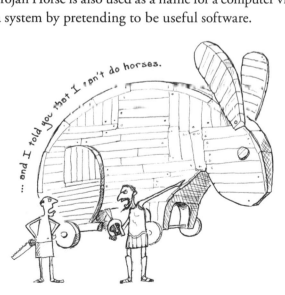

TYPHOON

A violent tropical storm or cyclone

Of the many monsters of Greek mythology, by far the greatest and most terrifying was the giant Typhon, whose name means whirlwind. The story is told that Typhon was hatched from two eggs, which had been coated in the semen of the Titan Cronus. When he was fully grown, his head touched the stars. When he stretched out his arms he could put one hand on the East and one hand on the West. On each hand he had dragons' heads instead of fingers, his eyes shot fire and below the waist he was girdled by hissing snakes.

Before long, Typhon had launched an attack on the gods on Mount Olympus. In the fury of his first assault, he seized Zeus and tore out his immortal tendons, leaving him as helpless as a child until Pan and Hermes managed to restore him to health. The battle continued across Greece, with Zeus hurling thunderbolts and Typhon hurling mountains until, finally, the giant was subdued.

The word typhoon is thought to have come to English from Typhon's name, but the modern meaning of the word was probably also influenced by the Chinese *tai fung* and the Arabic *tufan,* both meaning storm.

VANDAL

Someone who wantonly destroys or defaces property

The ancient Vandals were a Germanic tribe, one of several who crossed into Roman territory as the empire fell to pieces during the fifth century A.D. After crossing the Rhine into Roman Gaul, shortly after A.D. 400 the Vandals made their way slowly through France and Spain, causing severe destruction along the way. Eventually, during the 430s, the Vandals established a kingdom for themselves in the old Roman province of North Africa.

In 455 the Vandals achieved their greatest notoriety by sailing across the sea from Africa to sack the city of Rome. They weren't the first barbarians to break through the city walls. However, their sacking of the city was considered extremely violent and it ensured that their name would be remembered as a byword for wanton destruction.

VENEREAL DISEASE

A sexually transmitted infection

The word venereal is derived from the name of Venus, the Roman goddess of love. Venus was one of the most ancient gods of the

Roman Pantheon; she had been worshipped in Italy long before the city of Rome was founded. But as Rome fell more and more under Greek influence, Venus became regarded as the equivalent of the Greek goddess Aphrodite.

As the goddess of love and sex, Venus was always a popular figure whose annual festival was celebrated with equal vigor by matrons and prostitutes. The famous Julius Caesar, along with his adopted son, the emperor Augustus, even claimed the raunchy goddess as a divine ancestor. These proud Romans probably would have been heartbroken to discover that, after two thousand years, Venus's name would be best remembered as a word to describe diseases of the genitalia.

VOLCANIC ERUPTION

*A violent discharge of molten rock and hot gases
from beneath the Earth's crust*

The word volcanic comes from Vulcan, the name of the Roman god of fire and invention. Like Hephaestus, his more famous Greek equivalent, Vulcan was the blacksmith of the gods—a superb craftsman capable of manufacturing all sorts of technological wonders.

Despite his skills and power, Vulcan was sometimes a slightly pathetic figure on Olympus. He was short and had a limp, and compared to the other gods, with their tridents, thunderbolts and rippling divine muscles, he probably looked like a bit of a nerd. Once, in an argument, Jupiter picked Vulcan up by his legs and threw him right off Mount Olympus.

Vulcan didn't do that much better when it came to girls. He was married to Venus but she, of course, being the goddess of love, was constantly sleeping around. In particular, she carried on a long affair with Mars, who was incorrigibly masculine.

Perhaps unsurprisingly, Vulcan chose to spend most of his time locked away in his workshop which, like a James Bond villain's lair, was built in the middle of Mount Etna in Sicily. Whenever the volcano vented smoke and red-hot lava, the Romans knew that Vulcan was at work.

TO GO ON WINGED FEET

To travel with superhuman speed

Winged feet or sandals were the symbols of Hermes, the messenger of the Olympian gods and patron of traders and crossroads. He was known for cunning and trickery and, above all, for exceptional speed, which he gained with the help of a pair of miniature wings attached to his shoes. He even had a bonus pair of wings on his hat, in case he ever needed an extra boost.

Hoping, somewhat optimistically, to achieve Hermeslike efficiency in delivering messages, several of the world's postal services have since adopted the winged sandals as an emblem.

TO WORK LIKE A TROJAN

To work with great determination and endurance

In Greek mythology, the Trojans were the inhabitants of Troy, an important trading city on the coast of Turkey, not far from the mouth of the Black Sea. Troy was famous as the site of the Trojan War, a bloody siege that marked the end of the heroic age and provided the inspiration for Homer's epic poems, the *Iliad* and the *Odyssey*.

The conflict started when the Trojan prince Paris abducted Helen, the wife of King Menelaus of Sparta. Helen was the most beautiful woman in the world, and to get her back, Menelaus summoned his allies from all over Greece and set off to war.

THE HEROES AT TROY

GREEK

Achilles—a godlike mortal, invincible in battle but temperamental
Agamemnon—high king and ruler of Mycenae
Diomedes—great friend of Odysseus, brave enough to attack even the gods
Idomeneus—leader of the Cretans
Menelaus—king of Sparta and husband of the kidnapped Helen
Nestor—aged king of Pylos, better at talking than at fighting
Patroclus—Achilles' beloved companion
Odysseus—king of Ithaca, most cunning of the Greeks
Oilean Ajax—not as tough as Telamonian Ajax
Telamonian Ajax—strongest of the Greeks, a tower in battle

TROJANS

Aeneas—one of the only Trojans to survive, legendary ancestor of the Romans
Deiphobus—another of Hector's brothers (there were quite a few)
Hector—Priam's eldest son, strongest of the Trojans and loved by all
Memnon—a prince of Ethiopia
Paris—younger brother of Hector, vain and good with arrows (a womanly weapon)
Penthesilea—an Amazonian queen
Priam—aged king of Troy, past his prime
Sarpedon—captain of the Lycian allies, loved by Zeus

Arriving at Troy, the Greek alliance laid siege to the city, which was defended by the Trojans and their friends from the Turkish hinterland. In this clash of civilizations, the Greeks were the stronger side, boasting more men and greater heroes, including the fearsome Achilles. The Trojans, led by the sons of King Priam, fought against the odds with immense courage and determination—qualities that have been associated with Trojans ever since.

This legendary conflict is now thought to have some basis in historical fact. Excavations on the supposed site of Troy uncovered ruins of a city that showed signs of being captured and burned sometime during the thirteenth century B.C.—exactly when the Trojan War is thought to have taken place.

Z

ZEPHYR

A gentle breeze

In Greek mythology, Zephyr was the god of the benign West Wind and was thought to live in a cave somewhere in Thrace. Despite his supposedly gentle nature, Zephyr wasn't above the occasional act of divine violence. The most famous story tells of his love for a Spartan prince called Hyacinthus. Unluckily for him, the god Apollo had also fallen for the handsome youth.

Compared to Apollo, Zephyr was a very minor god, and Hyacinthus spurned his advances. In a jealous rage, Zephyr killed the boy by blowing a discus (a stone-throwing disc popular among Greek athletes) off course so that it struck him on the head. Heartbroken, Apollo turned the blood that flowed from Hyacinthus's wound into the flowers that still bear his name.

THE FOUR WINDS

Boreas—god of the North Wind that brings winter and cold

Eurus—god of the East Wind that brings misfortune

Notus—god of the South Wind that brings summer and storms

Zephyr—god of the West Wind that brings spring

SIGNS OF THE ZODIAC

Twelve astrological signs based on the twelve constellations of the ecliptic, which marks the path of the sun through the sky

It was astronomers in ancient Mesopotamia who first divided the ecliptic—the line along which the sun moves across the celestial sphere—into 12 sections, based on 12 constellations that are spread out along it. When the Greeks learned this system, they adopted it with enthusiasm, weaving it into their own mythology and calling it the *zôidiakos* (from the Greek word for animal).

Over the years, each of the twelve constellations of the zodiac became associated with a story or figure from Greek mythology:

Aries (The Ram)

Aries was thought to be the flying ram that rescued the twins Phrixus and Helle from the plotting of their cruel stepmother Ino. The ram carried Phrixus safely to King Aeëtes in Colchis, who was given the ram's famous golden fleece as a reward for his hospitality.

Taurus (The Bull)

The Greeks associated the constellation of Taurus with the myth of Europa, who was abducted by Zeus in the form of a giant white bull.

Gemini (The Twins)

The twins of Gemini were generally identified as the divine Dioscuri—Castor and Pollux. These twin brothers were the sons of Leda, brothers of Helen of Troy and Clytemnestra, and, after their deaths, became patron gods of sailors.

Cancer (The Crab)

Cancer is named after the crab that was sent by Hera to distract Heracles while he fought the Lernean Hydra. While the hero tried to defeat the Hydra's many heads, the crab nipped irritatingly at his heels and was rewarded with a place among the stars.

Leo (The Lion)

Leo was thought to be the Nemean Lion, a monstrous lion that had an impenetrable skin and was strangled by the hero Heracles for the first of his twelve labors.

Virgo (The Maiden)

Virgo was linked with a few mythological figures, most importantly the goddess Astraea, or Justice, who lived among men during the mythological Golden Age. After the advent of Christianity, Virgo came to be associated with the Virgin Mary.

Libra (The Scales)

These were the scales that were held by the goddess Justice to symbolize her impartiality.

Scorpio (The Scorpion)

Scorpio was the giant scorpion which famously killed the huntsman Orion when he offended the goddess Artemis. Both were transformed into constellations, and Scorpio can still be seen pursuing Orion across the skies.

Sagittarius (The Archer)

The archer of Sagittarius was generally thought to be one of the centaurs, a race of mythological beings who were half human and half horse.

Capricorn (The Sea-Goat)

Capricorn is a strange hybrid of a goat and a fish, sometimes associated with the goat-god Pan.

Aquarius (The Water Carrier)

Sometimes associated with Ganymede, a Trojan youth who was abducted by Zeus to be his immortal cup-bearer.

Pisces (The Fishes)

The sign of the fishes was sometimes associated with a myth about Aphrodite and Eros, who are said to have taken the form of fishes in order to escape from the giant Typhon.

INDEX

ENJOY THESE OTHER
READER'S DIGEST BESTSELLERS

I Used to Know That: Literature

Fun and interesting facts and quips about authors and books sure to delight the bibliophile and make anyone the life of hte party. Covering both modern and classicliterature, this book will interest both bookworms and trivia buffs.

C. Alan Joyce and Sarah Janssen

ISBN 978-1-60652-415-2

Spilling the Beans on the Cat's Pajamas

This book spills the beans on our best-loved euphemisms and most curious sayings, explaining their fascinating origins and the remarkable stories that surround them. It rounds up the usual suspects—the hundreds of catch phrases and expressions that enrich our everyday speech and makes them easy to find in an A-to-Z format.

Judy Parkinson

ISBN 978-1-60652-171-7

The Classics

From the Acropolis and Homer's *Odyssey* to "carpe diem" and Zeus. This book contains all the stuff you'd ever want to know about classical literature, language, philosophy, art, math, and more—without any of the stuffiness.

Caroline Taggart

ISBN 978-1-60652-132-8

A Certain "Je Ne Sais Quoi"

A smorgasbord of foreign words and phrases used in everyday English from Aficionado (Spanish) to Zeitgeist (German). Inside you'll find translations, definitions, and origins that will delight and amuse language lovers everywhere

Chloe Rhodes

ISBN 978-60652-057-4

I Used to Know That

Make learning fun again with these lighthearted pages that are packed with important theories, phrases, and those long-forgotten "rules" you once learned in school.

Caroline Taggart

ISBN 978-0-7621-0995-1

An Apple a Day

Discover the origins and meanings of proverbs—those colorful, time-honored truths that enrich our language and culture. You'll learn why these sayings have stood the test of time.

Caroline Taggart
ISBN 978-1-60652-191-5

i before e (except after c)

Featuring all the memory-jogging tips you'll ever need to know, this fun little book will help you recall hundreds of important facts using simple, easy-to-remember mnemonics from your school days.

Judy Parkinson
ISBN 978-0-7621-0917-3

I Used to Know That: Philosophy

Spanning over 2,000 years of philosophical thought, this book covers the main highlights, from Pythagoras to Socrates to Sartre. You'll get an overview of all the major theories, presented in an engaging format.

Lesley Levene
ISBN 978-1-60652-323-0

DON'T FORGET THESE BESTSELLERS

Easy as Pi

I Used to Know That: Geography

I Used to Know That: Shakespeare

Each Book is $14.95 hardcover

For more information visit us at RDTradePublishing.com

E-book editions also available.

Reader's Digest books can be purchased through retail and online bookstores. In the United States books are distributed by Penguin Group (USA), Inc. For more information or to order books, call 1-800-788-6262.